Chr. Dresser

People's Designer
1834 - 1904

Exhibition by New Century
2nd - 19th June 1999

Acknowledgments

The authors would like to thank the following for all their support and guidance:

Maureen Beesley, Dave Bonsall, Isobel Carew-Cox, Brian Cargin, Frances Collard, Roger Dodsworth, Pat Erridge, Elizabeth Forbes, Takeshi Furuya, Albert Gallichan, Robert Galt, Gilbert and George, Jim Gill, Joan Jones, Andrew McIntosh Patrick, Chris Morley, Barbara Morris, Jennifer Opie, Pat Paling, Linda Parry, Paul Reeves, Laurence Rogers, Peter Rose, John Scott, Ray Shaw, Matthew Skinner, Tom Skinner, Keiji Suzuki, Geoff Taffler, John Tierney, Lionel Towersey, EN Tunnicliffe, Tony Upton, Hilary Wade, Michael Whiteway

With grateful thanks to Steve Groves for Art Direction, New Century

With very many thanks to Debra Carew-Cox for the design of this book

Alastair Carew-Cox would like to thank John Azmat and all the staff at ICL Imaging for all their help and encouragement

Published by Alastair Carew-Cox, Home Farm, Abbots Morton, Worcestershire WR7 4NA. 01386 792 404

Printed in Great Britain by Swanhorse Colour Printers. 01905 775 127

Printed on Galerie Silk supplied by Alliance Papers, Birmingham. 0121 313 2111

ISBN 0 9532801 1 X

Front cover, *fig 1* Detail of a Carpet produced by John Lewis, Halifax. See fig 104
Title page, *fig 2* Detail of a Minton Vase. See fig 31
Back cover, *fig 176* Perry Ewer, possibly Toilet Jug.
The Perry attribution is based on a comparison of Perry and Benham and Froud items.   Cat. M-078

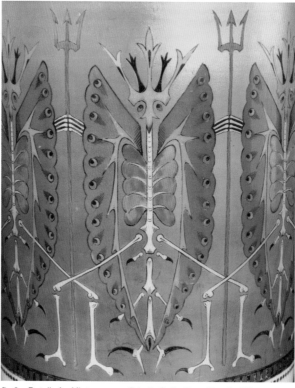

fig 3 Detail of a Minton vase. *Private Collection* (See fig 33)
fig 4, right Detail from Frog Suite wardrobe, Bushloe House

Foreword

by Barbara Morris

This exhibition and the accompanying publication is the fruit of five years' painstaking and meticulous research by Harry Lyons, with important contributions in the fields of glass and furniture by Christopher Morley. Both the exhibition and the book add considerably to our knowledge of the life and work of Dr. Christopher Dresser. Unknown objects have been discovered mis-attributions corrected and new avenues for further research opened up.

As Harry Lyons points out, although William Morris, an exact contemporary of Dresser, remains a household name to the present day with his textiles and wallpapers never being out of production, after his death in 1904 Dresser remained largely forgotten and virtually nothing was written about him. A brief mention in Nikolaus Pevsner's *Pioneers of Modern Design,* first published by Faber and Faber in 1936, followed by his article in *The Architectural Review* (vol. LXXXI, 1937) made little impact.

I first became aware of Christopher Dresser about 1950 during my research for the seminal exhibition of Victorian And Edwardian Decorative Arts at the Victoria and Albert Museum in 1952, organised by the late Peter Floud, Keeper of Circulation. Although Dresser's work was sparsely represented in the exhibition the display sparked off interest in Dresser on the part of collectors, (including Charles Handley-Read) dealers and museum curators. This interest escalated during the next two decades - with ever increasing prices for Dresser artifacts - and still shows no signs of waning. Such is the appetite for Dresser's works that there is a good deal of wishful thinking leading to some dubious attributions. Certain attribution is often difficult in the case of Dresser, partly because documentation has been destroyed or lost and also because it was normal practice in the 19th century for objects produced in a design studio to be marketed under the name of the head of the studio even if the object or pattern was produced by an assistant. In addition Dresser's publications of ornamental designs meant that they were there for all to use and adapt to their own purposes. Harry Lyons is to be congratulated in that he has scrupulously only attached a 'designed by Dresser' label to those objects that are either signed or fully documented and listed others as 'putative' or 'in the style of.' As Edward Lucie Smith wrote in *The Independent* (October 1st 1988) *"Today people are wearing designer labels outside their clothes, not inside them. So is it surprising that we are witnessing the triumph of the designer antique?"* But as Harry Lyons points out, we should not necessarily dismiss an object because it cannot be positively attributed - if it is good let it be appreciated in its own right.

The exhibition contains a marvellous array of objects, many hitherto unseen but to me the revelation of the exhibition is the 'carte de visite' portrait of Dresser himself. Up to now all we have known of his physical appearance was from a faded and blurred image of an old man sitting in his conservatory. Now we are confronted by the designer in his prime, a handsome man looking confidently at the camera, and we can believe in his dynamism and boundless energy.

fig 5, right   Carte de Visite Portrait of Christopher Dresser.   *Courtesy of the Linnean Society*

Introduction

by Harry Lyons

Quite simply, my reason for mounting this small exhibition is that I believe Christopher Dresser is one of the truly great design pioneers of our age. He aimed to bring good design into the homes of the population through articles of everyday household use at affordable prices. A reviewer of an exhibition by Dresser in 1876, reported:

> "... it is by bringing to the homes of the people objects of art and beauty at a low price that more good is done in refining the middle and lower classes than by all the museums in existence; the effect of the latter is transitory..." (*The Furniture Gazette* 20 May 1876)

To lift the national appreciation of good design, Dresser aimed at the mass of the population, not just the top two per cent. The progress of industrial revolution made such an aspiration feasible. Dresser wanted to surround people with items of good design. If for example, the toast rack you use everyday is functional and beautiful, you will react against something which is neither. The constant handling of such items will accustom the handler, consciously or subconsciously, to a high standard of design - a standard which will endure longer than any transitory experience.

This brings us to the sensitive issue of Dresser versus Morris. No remark by one about the other seems to have been recorded. Morris looked back to a romantic vision of the Middle Ages for answers; Dresser looked to his current surroundings and projected forward. As a member of the Morris Society (at least at the time of writing), I see no reason to denigrate Morris or Dresser at the other's expense. I do however, strive to echo Charles Holme, writing in 1898 from Morris's former home 'Red House' - that Morris was something of a cuckoo in the nest. The aims of the Arts and Crafts Movement should not begin and end with Morris.

Morris designed some 49 wallpapers in his lifetime. Dresser sold 30 wallpapers to one customer alone, en passant through Philadelphia. Why is Morris more revered than Dresser?

For a start, Morris had a successful shop selling his designs until 1940 - long after his death. Secondly Morris was identified as the icon of a craft movement which endures to this day. Thirdly, there is the political dimension which has established Morris as a hero in the socialist cause.

Clisby Kemp, writing on *Makers of the Modern Movement* in 1965, said

> "Morris was a medievalist, a sentimentalist, and an outrageous romantic, and, because, upper middle class liberals in Britain are possessed of these qualities in abundance, they have taken Morris to their hearts and made him a hero. And because most of our historians of economic, social and aesthetic change, came, until comparatively recently from that same class, Morris has been credited with many achievements for which he was not wholly responsible...."

These negative points about Morris have got to be made if other Victorian designers are to escape the shadow that the arbiters of design history have cast over the last one hundred years. My crib is against the arbiters, not Morris.

Dresser is all about design - innovative design. His competitors in this field were not Morris, nor the historiscists, they were Godwin and much later Mackintosh.

Quite simply, I believe that Dresser did more to ensure awareness of design in the objects 98 per cent of us use in our daily lives than anyone else. This awareness may have had even deeper effects on our overall art appreciation. The late Mervyn Levy (lecturer, broadcaster, writer, author and one time features editor of *The Studio*) wrote:

"...as early as 1879, the remarkable designer Dr Christopher Dresser anticipated the nature of Cubism - and Purism - in much of his work for (Dixons)... To my knowledge, no history of Cubism has ever made reference to the work of Dr Dresser and its clear relationship to the new aesthetic vision..." (M. Levy *Liberty Style,* 1986 page 3)

In the development of his argument quoted above, and one which would have delighted Dresser, Levy continued:

"The extent to which this new vision had its origins in the art of the designer rather than of the painter is often overlooked... running parallel but slightly ahead of the liberation of form in painting was the liberation of form in architecture and applied design... artists like Mackintosh, Voysey, Dresser and Archibald Knox were as important to the evolution and application of the new vision as were Picasso and Braque... only the narrow specialist can fail to relate the form/cleansing innovations of Knox and Picasso..."

Dresser gave two important lectures to the Royal Society of Arts - 'Ornamentation considered as High Art' in 1871, and 'Hindrances to the progress of Applied Art' in 1872. These lectures were to the point and stimulated discussion. In the first lecture, Dresser claimed equal status for ornamentation with the so-called Fine Arts,

"I claim for "ornamentation" that it is not simply art - that it is not Fine Art merely - but that it is High Art... it is symbolised imagination or emotion such as is calculated to teach some moral lesson or impress some important truth."

Dresser also made the point that many a follower of the Fine Arts was happy to have an expensive canvas on his walls surrounded with disappointing wallpaper, furniture and furnishings. Dresser would indeed have identified with Mervyn Levy.

Dresser had an uphill battle to assert himself. He was neither born a 'gentleman' nor was he a professional architect, unlike others in his field. He was forthright and attracted enemies easily through his outspoken comments. He had little time for the mediocre.

Some criticise Dresser for using the title 'Doctor' on the basis of an honorary degree. He was, nevertheless, empowered to use the title and any 'handle' to his name was probably an asset in Victorian England.

Dresser was a designer across the whole range of design. Many highlight his metalware, and others his ceramics. Both groups may be surprised to learn that these two aspects together cover only ten or fifteen per cent of his output. The bulk of his design work was in furnishings and textiles. If this small exhibition succeeds in bringing attention to aspects other than metal or ceramics, I will be content.

Harry Lyons
London
June 1999

Think of IKEA, Habitat, and Conran, in 1990s Britain, and what they all have in common - their customers expect good design at affordable prices. I am not talking about a world of expensive boutiques or workshops selling hand-crafted luxuries for millionaires, but the real world in which 98% of us live. If Christopher Dresser were alive today, he would gain some satisfaction from the existence of these successful shops catering for a clientele where expense is not the arbiter. The name of Christopher Dresser, however, is not one which receives much credit in the success of such shops.

In 1952, Peter Floud, the curator of the V&A Victorian Exhibition complained that the history of design jumped from 1830 to 1900, as though little other than William Morris had happened in the interim. This omission is still one which has not been fully corrected.

Christopher Dresser is the first designer to embrace industrial methods for the manufacture of household objects in any substantial sense. He created a design studio of professional designers as early as the mid-1860s. Dresser championed the doctrine of 'Form follows Function', decades before the Bauhaus and Modernist Schools took up the cry.[1] However, it is a phrase which has been hi-jacked by the Bauhaus and Modernist movements.

Early Years

Christopher Dresser was born in Glasgow on 4th July, 1834, the second son of an Excise officer. The work of Dresser senior required regular moves every four years or so [2] and it was in Bandon, County Cork, that Dresser claimed he received whatever schooling he had, during the four years his father was posted there. Dresser was just 13 years old when he enrolled in the School of Design at Somerset House, London.

Dresser's arrival at the School of Design in 1847 coincided with a sea-change in the philosophy of the school's ideals. There was an awareness that the school was not living up to its name. During Dresser's seven-year period as a student (1847-1854), Henry Cole [3] Richard Redgrave,[4] and George Wallis [5] steered the school towards acknowledging its needs and responsibilities to produce designers for industry, albeit with mixed success. Indeed many would blame these three for making the School of Design a Drawing School prior to its transformation into a teachers' college. Nevertheless, the young Christopher Dresser finished his time at the School with an acute awareness that design was a primary part of industrial production.

A further influence on the young Dresser would have been the movement for Design Reform, which found expression in Summerly's Art Manufactures. While Dresser may not have approved of this group's actual products, he would have sympathised with their motives. In the early part of Dresser's studentship, this group promoted the idea of good design for items of everyday household use. The leading figures in this movement were people whose names recur frequently in the life of Dresser - Henry Cole, Richard Redgrave, George Wallis, who were to form the 'powerhouse' in the Department of Science and Education, and its subordinate School of Design. Also included was John Bell the sculptor, who designed for Coalbrookdale. These are all names with whom Dresser would have had frequent contact as a student while at his most impressionable. They would have nurtured the belief in him that 'form follows function.'

The Great Exhibition of 1851, heightened awareness of the awfulness of British goods produced for household use, as a glance at *The Art Journal's* exhibition report will prove. Through the influence of luminaries such as Cole, Redgrave, Owen Jones, and Dr Semper, further impetus was given to the movement for promoting better design in industry. Dresser himself later pointed out, however, that of the three lecturers he studied with, in metalwork, ceramics, and textiles, only the ceramics lecturer had any practical experience.

A secondary result of the move to promote design was the encouragement given to industry to sponsor money prizes in the School of Design. I believe that this may have proved a crucial element in Dresser's career. Not only did he win prizes as a student, but later as a lecturer in the School of Design, he would have made some valuable contacts to be used in furthering his design career.

From at least 1849-1854, Dresser received scholarship money, which together with prize-money for his designs, should have provided him with some 50 pounds a year to supplement whatever his family may have provided. Nevertheless, whatever money he had, it was not sufficient to support a family.

Dresser married Thirza Perry on 24th May 1854, when he was 20 years old. His Cornish wife, four years his senior, was the daughter of a Methodist churchman,[6] and she was pregnant. Henry, their first-born son, arrived on 6th August, 1854, ten weeks after the wedding. Dresser chose to stand by his wife, and having done so, he needed money. On 17th June, 1854 Richard Redgrave signed a minute appointing Dresser to the Female School of Design as a lecturer on botany applied to ornament at £12-12-0 per annum. How Dresser survived on this money is difficult to imagine. His student days ceased in the Spring term of 1854, though his scholarship money may have continued.[7] However he may have managed, the events of 1854 were important in that Dresser embarked on a career in botany. There can be little doubt of a conscious change of course from an art-related career to botany. His marriage certificate records Dresser in May 1854, as an artist, the birth certificate of his first child records him as a botanist- a description of himself he kept until 1868.

Dresser as Botanist

In September 1855, Dresser's appointment as lecturer in Botany was confirmed and expanded. His appointment required a teaching commitment of six hours a week teaching at both the Central School and the Female School for £50 per annum. This salary was to be inclusive of costs involved in preparation and finding samples. The academic year was for 40 weeks - so Dresser had opportunities for pursuing private interests.

At first, Dresser's botanical career was in the context of botanical forms as applied to ornament. Dresser however, was not one to let events dictate a course to him. In 1856, Owen Jones invited Dresser to illustrate a plate on plants and flowers for his *Grammar of Ornament*. In 1857, Dresser at the age of 23, gave a lecture on ornamentation to the Royal Institution, and in the same year he patented a new invention, a method of reproducing images of leaves on the printed page, called *Nature Printing*.

In the same year, *The Art Journal* carried a series of 12 articles by Dresser on botany applied to art manufactures. In February 1858, Dresser also lectured the Royal Institution on a similar subject. In 1859, Dresser published two books on botany per se, They were *The Rudiments of Botany* dedicated to Dr Lyon Playfair [8] and *Unity in Variety*. The following year, 1860, Dresser published *The Popular Manual of Botany* described by Dresser as a *"Ladies' book"*. It was an attempt to simplify botany. The book avoided Latin names - reflecting his own difficulties in first studying botany.

Dresser's career in botany reached its climax in 1860. The 26-year-old Dresser had, a short time before been honoured with a doctorate by the University of Jena on the strength of two papers delivered to the Royal Institution.[9] Dresser was self-confident and was riding high and he had assembled an impressive folio of recommendations.

In early 1860, Dresser applied for and was appointed (though he was not first choice) to teach botany at the School of Medicine, St Mary's Hospital Paddington. He followed this up with a similar and successful application to teach botany at the London Hospital Medical College in July 1860 with references from Sir William Hooker and J.D. Hooker, the Director and Assistant Director, Kew Gardens and Dr J.H. Balfour, Professor of Botany at Edinburgh University. Later that year, Dresser applied for the Chair of Botany at University College London, an application which was unsuccessful. Dresser should not have been disappointed by this rejection. His own

(Footnote 1:   Dresser was not the first to adopt this cry of form and function-witness the American, Horatio Greenough in 1850 *Form and Function* edited by Harold A. Small.)

(Footnote 2:   Stockton 1839, London 1841, County Cork 1842, Hereford 1847 and Halifax 1852-1860.)

(Footnote 3:   Appointed Secretary to the Department of Practical Design 1851.)

(Footnote 4:   Headmaster of the Central School of Design, also writer of a report in 1851, on the state of the UK's industrial art.)

(Footnote 5:   Drawing Master of the School, later curator of the South Kensington Museum.)

(Footnote 6:   Thirza Perry's father William is given as 'City Missionary' in the marriage certificate. However, baptismal records of the Methodist (Wesleyan) church in Buddock, Falmouth, show William Perry as a farmer.)

(Footnote 7:   The annual report of the Department shows Dresser in receipt of his scholarship as at December 1854.)

(Footnote 8:   Lyon Playfair, a leading figure in the Department of Education, and later an MP was instrumental in founding the School of Mines, later Imperial College, and in 1857, moved to Edinburgh.)

(Footnote 9:   According to a letter to Pevsner from R. Rupenstein of Goettingen on 19th November 1936, Dresser was invited to be Ehrendoktor at Jena University, on the strength of the two papers. *Pevsner Archives*.)

academic record was not impressive. His teaching experience at the two Hospital Schools was of less than six months duration, and his experience of teaching Botany applied to art was for some five years only. Significantly, neither the Hookers nor Thomas Bell, President of the Linnean Society, were able to support his application for University College, being committed to another, the successful candidate.

fig 6   A botany teaching aid: Dresser.
Courtesy of the V&A Museum

Dresser's testimonials are of some interest. His Headmaster at South Kensington, R. Burchett, and his colleagues on the staff gave him warm support and referred to his ability to *"impart instruction."* His colleagues at St Marys also comment on Dresser's teaching as *"fluent, pleasing, clear and interesting."* (10)

Dresser was proposed for the Edinburgh Botanical Society and made a Fellow in January 1860. In November 1860, Dresser was proposed as a Fellow of the Linnean Society, the UK's leading Botanical Society and was elected in January 1861. Two of his proposers were Sir William and Joseph Hooker.

In the six years from June 1854, Dresser had made impressive progress in the field of Botany. He started out in the specific area of Botany applied to Art manufactures, and had extended this to Botany per se, leading to his appointment to lecture on Botany to two respected Medical Colleges. This five year period covered some very important developments including the publication of Charles Darwin's *Origin of the Species* in 1859. Dresser seemed to cling to traditional Christian beliefs in God as the creator of life, yet the implications of his botany books on the structure of plants and their adaptability to environment, closely paralleled what Darwin was proposing about natural selection of life on the Galapagos Islands. It is a puzzle unless one accepts that Dresser needed time to adapt his Methodist roots to his new circumstances. His folio of testimonials included two from Methodist clergymen, and Dresser may have found it politic not to be openly involved in the 'Darwinian' debate. At the time when his botany books were published, his career was firmly based in publicly funded teaching institutions and this may also have restrained his opinions. Whatever the reason, his expressions of piety in the belief of a single universal God sound unconvincing.

Dresser's botanical career finally ended in early 1868, when he gave his last lectures to the School of Design (now named the National Art Training School). Dresser's job description in 1863, was 'teacher of Botanical Drawing and Lecturer on Botany' for which he received a fixed sum of £20 per annum plus £61-13-4 for his share of fees. In 1867, he gave up his post at St Marys with minimum notice.(11) This period, of course, immediately predates the Paris Exhibition, 1867. In 1869, he also gave up his post at the London Hospital, somewhat abruptly, due it was said to 'illness'. Dresser retained his membership of the Linnean Society until 1881(12) and of the Edinburgh Botanical Society until his death.

In an effort to evaluate Dresser's standing as a Botanist, Robert Galt, Secretary of the Botanical Society of Scotland was invited to comment;

> *"Dresser's interest in plants was predominantly in the forms and designs which they display during growth. His theories were based on arguments which were unsupported by an adequate amount of evidence. He considered that a fundamental 'unity' occurred in the 'variety' of the Animal Kingdom; and that this confirmed the existence of a single God."*

Wherever history may place Dresser in the hierarchy of botany, one can at least claim that it was remarkable that in the first five years of his career, he should receive an honorary doctorate, and furthermore that Sir William Hooker was prepared to support the 26 year-old Dresser's application for the Chair of Botany at the London Hospital, and as a Fellow of the Linnean Society.

Dresser as Designer

Dresser wrote in 1871 *"that I was intended by nature as an artist, I doubt not."* [13] If one accepts that Dresser's excursion into Botany was the result of his personal circumstances in 1854, and not his natural choice it must have been something of a relief to become an "artist, ornamentist, architect" (each of these titles was used by Dresser). I have suggested 'designer' in the sub-title as a more accurate description of what Dresser did. Dresser was an artist only within certain limitations. He was an ornamentist certainly- but as for Dresser's claim to be an architect, I would suggest 'interior designer' as more accurate, he does not appear to have been a member of any Architectural Association, nor have I seen any evidence that Dresser had any schooling in the engineering aspect of Architecture. For example, the building and design of the Allangate extensions were carried out together with Horsfall, Wardle, Patchett, a firm of established Halifax architects.[14]

However, Dresser was something greater than anything suggested by his own epithets; he was a designer who thought through his designs. None of Dresser's own epithets would cover his designs for Hukin and Heath or Linthorpe, to take just two examples. The designs for these two companies are essentially shapes,[15] and are consciously 'form following function.' Moreover, by the late 1860s, he ran a design studio in the modern sense, which had a manager and apprentice designers.

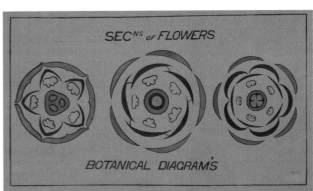

fig 7 A botany teaching aid: Dresser.
Courtesy of the V&A Museum

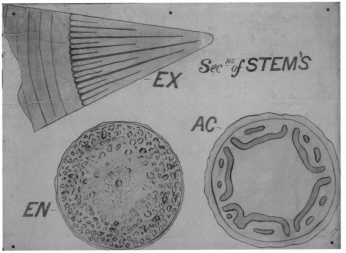

fig 8 A botany teaching aid: Dresser.
Courtesy of the V&A Museum

This is not simply an argument over words. It shows the development of Dresser from ornamentist to innovative full scale designer of household effects, pioneering new ground. The individuality shown in the Dresser metalware, glass, and in the ceramics for Linthorpe and Ault, all came in his later period, 1878-1896. In terms of design, Dresser was producing shapes and objects which hold their own against the Modernists 50 years later, and against Jensen, 70 years later.

(Footnote 10:   Botanical Society of Scotland Archives.)

(Footnote 11:   A board meeting of St Mary's on 30 April 1867, notes *"the pressure of increasing engagements but regrets that Dr Dresser has not made provision for the .. ensuing sessions ...* (and he is) *honour-bound to arrange the courses..."*)

(Footnote 12:   Dresser then became in arrears of some seven years' annual subscription.)

(Footnote 13:   *RSA Journal* 1871, p.352.)

(Footnote 14:   The original house extension plan is in a private collection.)

(Footnote 15:   *Pevsner archives.*)

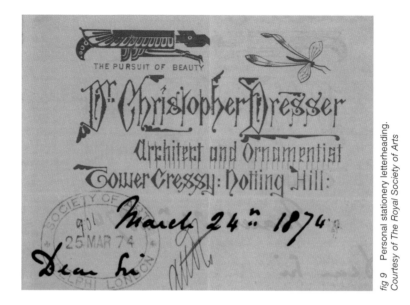

fig 9   Personal stationery letterheading.
Courtesy of The Royal Society of Arts

Dresser as ornamentist

1847-1861

The first recorded money that Dresser earned for his designs was as a student at the School of Design in 1851/52, when he won prizes for a tea, a breakfast and a dessert service, and a further prize for a design on silk, making a total of £6 in prize money. Dresser won further medals at the School in textile design, one of these designs being printed.

Serious money did not accrue until the period preceding the International Exhibition, London, 1862. There is little evidence to fill in the gap between 1854-1861, but I would be surprised if Dresser were not engaged in some form of design work. It is clear that he was close to Owen Jones, and there is a cryptic comment in a file note in the Victoria and Albert Museum records for 1905, by the then Director of the Museum that Dresser "worked with Owen Jones in the sixties." [16] Certainly Dresser's ecstasy over Jones' work at St James' Hall, and the Crystal Palace could be seen in the context of a work association. Dresser's short lived lecturing engagement as a 'Professor of Ornamental Art and Botany' in the Crystal Palace [17] may also have covered this period. That Dresser was earning money over and above his official lecturing engagements through his literary contributions to learned societies and *The Art Journal* is probable. Dresser's first two books on Botany were reprinted, suggesting good sales (and income). Moreover, while he had a steadily increasing family, he was able to travel abroad and could afford to move upmarket into a comfortable terrace house with garden in the North End Road, Hammersmith,[18] to accommodate his children and a living-in servant. I would guess that Dresser, ever one to use any opportunity, was exploiting contacts in industry through his association with the South Kensington School and Museum, as well as Owen Jones' contacts in trade and industry. We also know that Dresser promoted himself and his designs around the country visiting trade outlets and industry.[19] Dresser was not a full time member of the teaching staff of any institution, and what with the long academic holidays and the practice of paying others to teach occasionally in his place,[20] he had plenty of time to travel and tout his designs.

1862-1876

This period represents the expansion of Dresser's ornamentation and design work from a one-man part-time operation to a permanent and full-time studio, perhaps the first ever studio of its kind which existed to create and sell designs to industry. This studio may have employed up to ten people.[21] The work was essentially one of creating originals and should not be confused with the Victorian profession of pattern drawer whose job was largely to work out a pattern from a customer's sketch or requirements.

Dresser claimed in 1862, that his literary work was being *"repeatedly interrupted by manufacturers of the greatest eminence desiring designs for the London Exhibition."* [22] I have not seen any direct credits to Dresser in reports of the Exhibition, but his claim seems likely. He certainly seems to have produced designs for Minton for one.[23] This exhibition was important to Dresser as a vehicle for his design work, and the publication of his guide to the Exhibition. Although it is frustrating not to know who else Dresser may have designed for in 1862, the International Exhibition had one unexpected but significant effect on Dresser, in that it opened his eyes to the delights of Japanese ornamentation. It is likely that Dresser would have seen Japanese artifacts before 1862, but the collection assembled by Sir Rutherford Alcock, a British Ambassador to Japan, was put together by a discerning eye and someone who knew Japan well. Obviously, Dresser discussed the collection at length with Alcock while he, Dresser, was buying items and making some 80 drawings of the remaining parts of the collection.[24] Dresser's fascination was destined to lead on to his association with the import firm of Londos and his visit to Japan in early 1877.

Meanwhile, Dresser was building on his design work. In 1865, there was an exhibition in Liverpool which included some of Dresser's wallpaper designs [25] and an examination of the Patent Office Design Registry (PODR) records for this period, show some probable Dresser designs registered by William Cooke, a wallpaper manufacturer. Dresser is also noted by *The Building News* as a designer for wallpaper and carpets.[25]

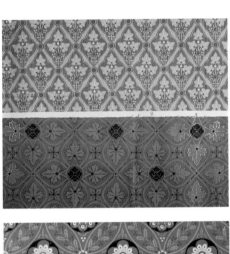

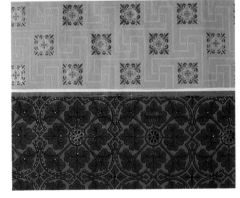

figs 10,11,12 & 13 Wallpapers registered at the PODR by William Cooke, 1863 - 65. Courtesy of the PRO

(Footnote 16:   The file note is in the context of whether the V&A should buy some of Owen Jones' sketches from Dresser's estate.)

(Footnote 17:   See the title page of *The Art of Decorative Design,* 1862.)

(Footnote 18:   2, Myrtle Place, North End Road, now demolished. He moved there in early 1862.)

(Footnote 19:   Dresser's letter to the *The Furniture Gazette;* 24 July 1875.)

(Footnote 20:   Minutes of the Royal London Hospital Board MC/A/1/2 pp 79, 88, 95 of 1869/1870.)

(Footnote 21:   Durant, *Christopher Dresser* p.41, Frederick Burrow's recollections.)

(Footnote 22:   *The Art of Decorative Design,* Preface.)

(Footnote 23:   Joan Jones *Minton* p.56.)

(Footnote 24:   *RSA Journal,* February 1878, p.169.)

(Footnote 25:   *The Building News.* 21 April 1865.)

fig 14   Design for *The Building News* c.1869 from Dresser headed 'for Mr Smith' from the Moyr Smith archive.   *Courtesy of The Potteries Museum & Art Gallery*

Also, around about 1865, Dresser executed his first recorded interior design scheme, for J. Ward of Halifax,[26] the only recorded detail is that of the dining room. The sketch, however, in black and white, cannot convey any idea of the overall room effect, colour being crucial to the 'Dresser effect.'

The momentum of activity in the Dresser studio would have been greatly accelerating at this stage. We know from George Augustus Sala [27] that many British and European exhibits at the Paris Exhibition, 1867, were from the Dresser studio and this would have probably meant a 'lead-time' of some two years between design and production. Furthermore, we know from John Moyr Smith's article in *The Biographer* that when he took 'temporary service' in the Dresser Studio [28] in early 1867, he *"made some thousands of designs for ironwork, furniture, pottery, wallpapers, lace curtains, carpets, decorations and kindred works ."* Whatever the exact dates or length of time, Moyr Smith paints a picture of hectic activity. From the designs that can be identified at the Paris Exhibition, 1867, Dresser-designed exhibits would have included Minton, Wedgwood in ceramics, and Brinton & Lewis in carpets. By Sala's account, Dresser was designing for both British and continental manufacturers and his reputation would have been high amongst exhibiting companies. About this time, he would have started designing cast iron for Coalbrookdale, but I cannot ascertain for whom he designed the lace and furniture that Moyr Smith writes of. One or more of the numerous lace manufacturers around Calais or Nottingham are possible candidates for lace,[29] and in furniture, probably Lamb or Ogden,[30] both of Manchester (see fig 15) and Constantine of Leeds.[31]

fig 15   Cabinet labelled 'Ogden'. c. 1867.   *Courtesy of Andrew McIntosh Patrick*

The best documented 'interior design scheme' of Dresser is Allangate, Halifax, the house of Thomas Shaw MP. Allangate is discussed in more detail elsewhere, but a mention is relevant here. It would make sense that furniture, wallpapers, carpets and textiles would have been specially commissioned for Allangate. As best I can, I estimate the development of Allangate to have been 1869-70. Allangate would however have been only one of several decorative commissions, details and identities of which are now probably lost to us.

The Lister Archive [32] holds some correspondence from 1869 onwards between Dresser and John Lister over the decoration of a chapel which gives an insight into Dresser's working. He would also have done a decorative scheme for John Lewis [33] at Savile Hall, Halifax at this time. These, sadly with Bushloe House, Leicester are only four or so of the decorative schemes we know about and only Allangate remains in any significant way. Most of Bushloe House has been demolished and the other two completely destroyed.

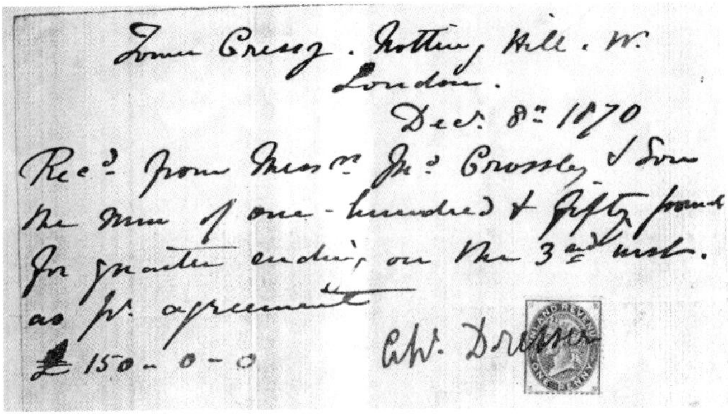
Tower Cressy. Notting Hill. W.
London.
Dec. 8th 1870
Recd from Messrs Jno Crossley & Sons
the sum of one-hundred & fifty pounds
for quarter ending on the 3rd inst.
as per agreement
£150 - 0 - 0 Chr. Dresser

fig 16 Receipt for quarter payment from Dresser to Crossleys.
Courtesy of Crossley Archive at Halifax Local Studies

The importance of these schemes in Dresser's career is the prestige and the 'shop window' which they provided for his talents. Equally important, however, is the 'clout' they would have given Dresser in approaching manufacturers to commission items.[33] Nowhere more so, than with John Crossley, the Halifax carpet manufacturer. Crossleys had their own staff designers, but I imagine the influence of John Lewis (ex Brinton & Lewis) with his uncles, the Crossley brothers, together with Dresser's own ability to commission carpets for his interior designs may have been responsible for Dresser's contract with the Crossleys. The receipt, (see fig 16) suggests that Crossleys was one of the companies with whom Dresser had a term contract (maybe three years), on the lines of his contract with William Ault. The fee does not seem extravagant for an exclusive contract and compares with Dresser's claims that his services could be secured for the salary of a staff designer.

Dresser became a rich man during this period. In late 1868 Dresser moved into a six-story Italianate house with gardens in Campden Hill, London.[34] In 1868, he also had the confidence to cut his botany career, which he plainly had maintained as a 'fall-back' option. Dresser was well-known to manufacturers of household effects as a good designer. His designs were sold by leading manufacturers, a list of names which endured well into the 20th century.

Dresser's design success gave him confidence. He was elected a member of the Royal Society of Arts in December 1870,[35] and he gave several lectures there over the next ten years during which he remained a member. Dresser was also known as a writer for the provincial newspapers, a contributor to professional and trade publications, and he produced five respected books on design which were well regarded.[36]

Dresser had a burning passion to promote the cause of good design. I believe it was a genuine passion and it was the reason he would lecture to learned bodies and trade organisations such as at the Whitby jet workers, without fee. He wanted to improve the perception of good design and good taste by bringing design into objects of everyday household use,[37] and to as wide a cross-section of the population as possible. For this reason, he claimed that his name on a wallpaper selvage by Jeffreys in 1874 was a guarantee that it had 'art' value, (see fig 17.) Was this 'big-headed,' self-promoting or genuine? I imagine all three factors played a role in this action, but I have no doubt that altruism was a significant factor.

(Footnote 26: *The Furniture Gazette* 17 June, 1880.)

(Footnote 27: G.A. Sala *Notes and Sketches of the Paris Exhibition* 1867.)

(Footnote 28: *The Biographer,* Vol. IX, p.97, October 1894. The life of Moyr Smith is presumed to have been written or ghosted by Moyr Smith. Moyr Smith does not mention Dresser by name, but I have little doubt about the identity.)

(Footnote 29: A glance through the PODR archives, BT43 and BT44, show no obvious Dresser pattern, but those from Calais seem the most likely.)

(Footnote 30: See *The Ipswich Sketch Book.*)

(Footnote 31: The Shaw family house at Holywell Green was furnished from this source. *Private family archive.*)

(Footnote 32: *Lister Archive,* Halifax.)

(Footnote 33: John Lewis left Brinton & Lewis 1869 to join his uncles on the Board of Crossley until 1871, when he founded his own company in Halifax.)

(Footnote 34: Five storeys and a basement. Then as now, a smart address. Dresser's 11th child Effie was born here on 19th February, 1869.)

(Footnote 35: One of his first magnanimous gestures was to donate £25 to an RSA fund to encourage music.)

(Footnote 36: *The Art of Decorative Design* 1862, *Development of Ornamental Art in the International Exhibition,* London 1862, *Principles of Design,* 1873, *Studies in Design,* 1876 and *Modern Ornamentation,* 1886.)

(Footnote 37: The second of the three 'Philadelphia Lectures' to the Pennsylvania Museum, *Penn Monthly* February 1877 p.144. *"If you ask* (Minton and Elkington) *what their wealth sprang from, it will be found to be from the production of useful objects rather than from ... great art works."*)

fig 17   A page from *The Jeffreys' Workbooks* c.1874.
Note the selvage on the bottom page, carrying Dresser's name. *Courtesy of A. Sanderson and Sons*

Circa 1872, a City importing firm of 'art manufactures,' acquired Dresser's services as 'art advisor.' This firm, Charles Reynolds and Co. imported 'fancy objects' from Europe and from the cheaper end of the Japanese market. According to Dresser [38] he persuaded the company to expand the existing Japanese business so as to include the best art products, while still maintaining its presence in the cheaper end of the market. This new business eventually became Londos & Co. at the Art City Warehouse, 126 and 127 London Wall, in the City of London. The Art City Warehouse sold only to the wholesale market, and when an exhibition of its goods was held in May 1876, *The Furniture Gazette* reporter was surprised to find the warehouses fitted out and decorated in a manner intended to display Londos' goods in appropriate settings.[39] The manner of presentation, attributed solely to Dresser, was against the inclination of the owners, but so successful was the venture that the business expanded into the neighbouring warehouse. The report in *The Furniture Gazette* gives a good idea of how Dresser saw his 'mission.' The display was divided into four parts, covering antique products of the Orient; modern products of the Orient; French art manufacturers especially ceramics by Theodore Deck and glass by Phillipe Brocard,[40] which were inspired by Asia; and finally replicas of medieval brass work. The affordability of many of the Oriental imports was stressed, with items on sale from one penny upwards. Dresser's motives shone through even more clearly in the following excerpt.

> "It is by bringing to the homes of the people, objects of Art and beauty at a low price that more good is done in refining the middle and lower classes than by all the museums in existence. The effect of the latter is transitory, while that of the former is to a certain extent, permanent." (*The Furniture Gazette* 20 May 1876)

Alexandra Palace

One should not leave this period of Dresser's life without reference to his Alexandra Palace involvement. The Palace at Muswell Hill was first opened in the early 1860s as North London's answer to the Crystal Palace. After a chequered history, including a fire in 1873, a determined effort to boost the enterprise was made,[41] when Dresser was appointed Art Advisor to the Alexandra Palace Company. It was planned to include permanent exhibits of an international character such as a Japanese village, a Moorish house, and an Egyptian house. Details are somewhat sketchy, but it would appear [42] that the "entire Japanese colony" at the Vienna, 1873 exhibition was secured for the company, as was a Moorish house, two Moorish courts, and several other foreign exhibits. The decoration of the exhibit was in the hands of Henry Tooth.[43] Obviously, Dresser was enthusiastic, and *The Furniture Gazette* [44] equally enthusiastically reported a preview of the Moorish and Egyptian houses for the management committee:

> "After the committee had been conducted over the houses... the party returned and seating themselves on elaborately embroidered cushions in the divan of the Egyptian villa, were supplied with scarves and turbans, and enjoyed amazingly, the native pipes, cigarettes, and that delightful coffee .... handed round on beautifully wrought trays by Mr Churcher [45] and the students of Dr Dresser, who, (were) arrayed as Moors and Egyptians......... Mr Churcher, private secretary to Dr Dresser, had the advantage of a long stay in Morocco where he ..... collected art material ... (also) Mr Caspar Clarke [46] who had been to Cairo for a similar purpose. ..."

It was such enthusiasm for his task as the above excerpt shows, that set Dresser apart from his contemporaries, and emphasises the impression that his mission for 'the truth in art' was paramount amongst his motives for

(Footnote 38:   *The RSA Journal* 1878 p.170.)

(Footnote 39:   Pots on furniture, in something approximating to room settings, *The Furniture Gazette* 20th May 1876.)

(Footnote 40:   Ibid. The whole of the consignments of these two well-known firms being taken by the Art City Warehouses.)

(Footnote 41:   Sir Edward Lee was appointed in overall charge. He had been the Director of the Dublin International Exhibition, 1871 and was destined to be the future manager of the Art Furnishers' Alliance.)

(Footnote 42:   *The RSA Journal,* 12 September 1873.)

(Footnote 43:   From Ryde, Isle of Wight. Later manager of the Linthorpe pottery, before founding his own Bretby pottery in 1883.)

(Footnote 44:   *The Furniture Gazette* 2 May, 1874, p.426.)

(Footnote 45:   Churcher was Dresser's office manager.)

(Footnote 46:   Caspar Clarke was not a direct employee of Dresser, and seems to have been employed by the South Kensington Museum.)

spreading the gospel of good design. The Palace and grounds did not open formally until May 1875. By this time, the Japanese village brought from Vienna was in place. In the main hall of the Palace, household goods were exhibited at a bazaar, and included Dresser's designs for Jeffrey's wallpapers which carried his name. Altogether, displays showing household goods and portrayal of domestic life made up a sizeable portion of the Palace Exhibition, including an exhibit by Jackson & Graham. *The Illustrated London News* drew attention to the 'domestic' interiors of the Moorish, Egyptian and Japanese exhibits.

However, by now, Dresser implementing his belief in good design for all, was launching his exhibition at the City Art Warehouse, and preparing for his visit to Japan.

1876-1882

This period represents the highest and lowest points of Dresser's fortunes. I also believe this period saw some of the best of Dresser's creative genius, but it has to be seen in the context of a bubbling enthusiasm, and a less than sound commercial judgement.

In October 1876, Dresser left the UK to attend the Philadelphia Centennial Exhibition, continuing on to Japan. Due to the pressure of work, Dresser had already declined an invitation to sit on the ceramics jury, but the prestige of these international gatherings was such that Dresser found value in meeting people and keeping abreast of world developments in design. During his stay in the USA, he was commissioned, through Londos, to buy a collection of Japanese art items for Tiffany and Co., New York. Dresser also visited the wallpaper manufacturers Wilson & Fennimore, Philadelphia, where he supervised the production of 30 designs for ceiling papers and wall papers. He also gave three lectures in Philadelphia, seemingly with the encouragement of Cunliffe-Owen, on the ideals of a museum, art schools, and art manufactures. Importantly, Dresser also made valuable contact with the head of the Japanese Commission at the Exhibition, General Saigo, who was to prove a true friend. Little else about his visit is known, but he seems to have struck a rapport with Americans. A New York Times columnist referred to him affectionately as 'The Doctor' and described him as;

> "... a full-grown Cockney, black of beard, bright of eye, and who would talk a man into a state which American ingenuity illustrated some time ago by a skeleton in a deal box; but his chat is charming...."
> (*New York Times* 6 May 1877)

Dresser met up with General Saigo and his team in San Francisco and arrived in Japan on Boxing Day, 1876. The main reason for Dresser's visit to Japan was in his role as art advisor to Londos which required Dresser to make a collection of Japanese art wares for shipment back to the UK. However, his friend Cunliffe Owen asked him to take this opportunity to organise a collection of British and European art manufactures as a gift to the Japanese.[47]

It was a momentous visit to Japan, probably due to the influence of General Saigo. Dresser was presented to the Emperor and handed over his collection of European Art manufactures. The Emperor thanked Dresser and invited him to tour Japan as his guest, giving him unfettered access to the Imperial Collections. Dresser seemed to have taken full advantage of the invitation and with a true professional's interest in his subject, took extensive notes and asked questions. There seems little doubt that his infectious enthusiasm struck a chord with the Japanese, as it had earlier in America.

We know that Dresser formed the Londos and Tiffany collections, and the Londos office in Yokohama would have dispatched them. Of longer term plans, while in Japan, we have little knowledge. It is not possible to say whether Dresser had any idea of forming the company Dresser & Holme at this stage, but on balance the idea probably came later. The following year, February 1878, Dresser's 20 year-old son, Christopher, arrived in Yokohama as a member of the Londos staff, which would suggest amiable relations between Dresser and Londos.[48]

Dresser left Japan in early April 1877, and returned westwards via the Suez Canal.[49] He stopped over in Hong Kong on 10 April, and made an excursion to Canton, at which place Londos also had a depot. This excursion seems to have been brief because he is next traced leaving Singapore on 26 April, 1877.[50] His return journey took him to Ceylon, Aden, the Suez Canal ports and Naples, before taking the train from Marseilles north to the French channel ports. Dresser probably arrived back in London sometime in June, 1877. The next occasion on which we can trace Dresser is 4 July, 1877, when he begs Sala, following a night 'on the town,' to promote Japanese lacquer work through his various press outlets. Sala duly obliged as best he could, but in an indirect way in *The Illustrated London News.*[51]

> *"A dear friend of mine, who has just come from a journey round the world... (has given me a lacquer table with) legs three inches long..."*

In *The Daily Telegraph* [52] Sala gives Dresser further mentions but in a more direct way.

Little is known of Dresser's activity in the aftermath of his return from Japan, but he would have been engaged in exploiting his Japan connections on behalf of Londos, and/or his private venture with Charles Holme, 'Dresser and Holme.' His son Christopher left London for Yokohama in December 1877, which Dresser said in a letter to Sala, had kept him busy. Dresser must have also given some considerable attention to his design contract with Hukin and Heath which would have commenced soon after his return from Japan. He also would have been thinking out his concept of an 'art industry' complex in Linthorpe with John Harrison.

The year 1878 saw evidence of hectic activity by Dresser. He arranged an exhibition of a Japanese ceiling, sent to him on the orders of the Emperor of Japan.[53] He volunteered to the Royal Society of Arts to give a lecture on Japan, and did so in February 1878. Never one to aim low, he suggested HRH the Duke of Edinburgh as a suitable chairman for his lecture, but eventually settled on Sir Rutherford Alcock. Also at this time he claimed to have briefed the Prince and Princess of Wales about Japanese art objects [54] and he later designed carved lattice-panels, stained black on a coloured background for the smoking-room of the Prince of Wales' pavilion at the Paris Exhibition, 1878.[55]

Dresser & Holme opened its doors in June 1879. The circumstances leading to the establishment of Dresser & Holme is uncertain as is the relationship, if any, it held with Londos.[56] The setting up of Dresser & Holme must have entailed work over a lengthy period. *The Furniture Gazette* rhapsodised over the display.

> *"From the moment we entered, we seemed to have left England and to have been transported to Japan, so completely orientalised was everything around; the building with inlaid tiles of various colours and exquisite design completely covering the walls, the ceilings ... the plants in large pots, the carpets and cane easy-chairs, all gave a cheerful, homelike effect......"*

Dresser, true to his belief that items of good design need not be expensive, presented the collection. Items from the Orient, particularly Japan, India, China and Persia were presented in three separate parts. Firstly, the cheap end of the market which was the most extensive department, making yet again, the point of 'affordability.' The second part of the collection represented items of 'special artistic merit,' and presumably were more expensive. Finally, a third section devoted to 'antiques' of the Orient and India.

(Footnote 47:   This is explained in detail later in the text.)

(Footnote 48:   *Japan Directory,* 1879 shows Christopher Dresser (Junior) accredited to Londos, Yokohama as a clerk.)

(Footnote 49:   He did not return via New York with the Tiffany collection as stated in the two books on Dresser.)

(Footnote 50:   *Singapore Daily Times* 26 April 1877.)

(Footnote 51:   *Illustrated London News,* 4 August 1877.)

(Footnote 52:   *Daily Telegraph,* 12 December 1877.)

(Footnote 53:   Four such ceilings were sent, of which one was exhibited in a furnished room setting in Streeter's, 18 New Bond Street, London *The Furniture Gazette* 15 June 1878.)

(Footnote 54:   Letter of 28 December 1877, to the RSA.)

(Footnote 55:   Dresser later attended the Paris Exhibition as a juror in the wallpaper section, but the comparative absence of comment by him on this exhibition - compared to the other large international exhibitions - suggests he was pre-occupied with other matters.)

(Footnote 56:   *The Furniture Gazette,* 12 July 1879, p.22 in an article on Dresser & Holme, however, records that *"Dr Dresser's son is still in Japan, and is engaged with* (others) *travelling through the country."*)

Dresser & Holme, like Londos, was an import company and the goods that were displayed, as with the City Art Warehouse exhibition of 1876, were for wholesale purchasers only. The display reflected Dresser's Japanese pre-occupation together with the Indian based interests of Charles Holme, a collection of which items Holme had already exhibited at Paris in 1878 under the umbrella of his father's firm.

The period 1877-1882 saw some of the very best of Dresser's designs. Dresser, if thought to be somewhat eccentric was well-regarded by the country at large through his books, his forthright views, and his visit to Japan. He also had a wide audience in Europe and America. He was a desirable contact for any progressive manufacturer wanting to produce new innovative and affordable household goods to an increasingly large population. Designs from this period can be seen elsewhere in this catalogue, particularly those for Hukin & Heath, Dixon and Linthorpe. Dresser had the authority and power to push through his designs, and manufacturers seemed to acquiesce in the belief that Dresser was 'probably right'. However, he was simply ahead of his time. Consumers and manufacturers both needed time to appreciate what Dresser was trying to achieve.

'Form follows function' was not a principle that could be adopted overnight by consumers used to heavily decorated and traditional shapes. The designs and decorations previously associated with Dresser were more easily understood by the consumer. For example, Dresser's designs for Minton and Wedgwood were colourful and had interesting decoration but were not revolutionary. The designs for Linthorpe, Hukin & Heath and Dixon relied on shape and colour and any decoration, where used, was muted.

The designs for this period are different from those he produced before he went to Japan. It is an interesting point to ponder, whether the 1880's metal and ceramics designs were the logical end object of his earlier work, or whether his visit to Japan had changed his concepts. I believe the latter. There is not much more to say regarding this, as the products of this period speak for themselves. However, one must be cautious in distinguishing what is pure Dresser, and what has been compromised to meet manufacturers' qualms about marketability. Many collectors of Dresser, seek Modernism and Bauhaus features in Dresser's designs. To such collectors, only shape, and colour (in ceramics) matter. Even Japanese decoration is eschewed by such collectors. Nevertheless, I can understand that manufacturers were reluctant to accept Dresser's innovative designs without some 'sweetener' to the consumer, in the form of decoration as a relief to the rather stark shapes. Decoration by Dresser was added in many cases and was suitable but presumably more expensive. Later decoration, without Dresser's supervision is a much different matter.

As Dresser's connection with, say, Linthorpe ceased, cost-effective management pandered ever more to the public taste for decoration. The Linthorpe pieces of 1882 and after, show an increasing predilection for naturalistic flowers, and less angular shapes. The same happened with Hukin & Heath and Dixon in the 1880s, and with Ault patterns after 1895.

Apart from running a busy studio, a large part of Dresser's time must have been spent in 1878 and 1879 'fleshing out' the concept of an 'art manufactures' complex at Linthorpe with John Harrison. Harrison provided the funds and backing for Linthorpe and his prospectus clearly stated that ceramics, wallpaper and glass would be produced here.[57] Dresser was described as Art Superintendent, and it is he who would have selected Henry Tooth to manage the project. Henry Tooth, the son of a butcher had impressed Dresser whom he had stumbled across in Ryde, Isle of Wight, while Tooth was using Dresser's designs to decorate the local Town Hall.

Although many of the workers at Linthorpe were unable to remember Dresser ever having visited the pottery, it is probable that they were referring to the period when full-scale production started, by which time Tooth was well ensconced. It is difficult to imagine Dresser not visiting Linthorpe at all during the period 1877-1879. Although only the ceramics part of the operation prospered, some work was carried out on both wallpapers [58] and glass.[59]

In addition to all this activity, Dresser was involved with ambitious projects for Hukin & Heath, over and above contributing his own startlingly original designs. The description of Hukin & Heath's opening exhibition in August 1879, at their new London premises in the City clearly shows the hand of Dresser and suggests an enormous amount of pre-exhibition activity.

A fuller assessment of Dresser's own metal designs can be gathered later in the text, but it would seem that Dresser was active in other areas. Hukin & Heath showed off a collection of Persian and Cashmere metal covered with gold and silver which was manufactured by *"native workmen, who are expressly and exclusively employed by the firm."* [60] In addition, Japanese metalware was exhibited along with a collection of 'the new Linthorpe' ware mounted in the firm's silver. Some Doulton and oriental wares were similarly mounted. It is difficult not to see the guiding hand of Dresser in this exhibition.

However, there may have been some tension between Hukin & Heath and Dresser, because Dresser seems to have started designing for J. Dixon & Sons in late 1879. The first recorded metal designs for J. Dixon appear in Dixon's Design workbooks dated 1879. Presumably, this is late 1879 as the Hukin & Heath exhibition in London in August 1879 made reference to Dresser as still with the firm.[61] The first Dixon designs of 1879, are the well-known 'one-off' tea-pot designs which were then as now, eccentric, and may have been too much for Hukin & Heath.

Were this workload not sufficient, we learn that the weekly, *The Furniture Gazette* engaged Dresser, beginning January 1880, as its art-editor. 1880 was a year which tested Dresser's stamina to the full and it is hardly surprising that something had to give. The commitment to write weekly articles for *The Furniture Gazette* in his role as art-editor, and presumably to lend his authority to all aspects of the magazine must have been the ultimate drain on Dresser's health. The first six months of 1880, saw a sizeable input by Dresser into the magazine, but from July onwards the input dwindles until the announcement of Dresser's resignation in the last issue of 1880.

November 1880, also saw the launch of the Art Furnisher's Alliance [62] at 157 New Bond Street (the block in which the French company, 'Hermes' now stands). The modest note in *The Furniture Gazette* announcing the opening, contrasts with the fanfare promoting the launch and formal offer to shareholders in June 1880. The muted launch taken with the paucity of Dresser's input into *The Furniture Gazette*, suggests the strain of this workload laid Dresser low by late 1880. He may well also have been suffering financial strain. It seems odd that Dresser should have been the holder of one single £5 share in the Art Furnisher's Alliance, were he otherwise than financially 'stretched'. Moreover, 1880/81 is the last year in which he was a paid up member of the Royal Society of Arts and of the Linnean Society. From the preface to *Japan* written in August 1881, we learn that Dresser suffered a long and painful illness. Whether the illness was the cause, or the result of the downturn in his finances, we do not now know, but between ill health and financial problems he was obliged to sell his large freehold house in Campden Hill and take on the lease of Wellesley Lodge, Sutton in 1882.[63] Sutton was not grand like Campden Hill and one inevitably associates Sutton with Pooterland in *Diary of a Nobody* as a commuter suburb of white collar workers and clerks.

Dresser simply overreached himself. From a straightforward design studio, Dresser grew to be a man with a mission to bring well-designed articles into every class of household in the land. To this end he involved himself in establishing commercial ventures which would blast society into appreciating good design. This enthusiastic urge may have been controlled while he worked for companies such as Londos, but in the case of Dresser & Holme, in which he was a joint owner, an important restraint to his enthusiasm may have been removed. When the national economic downturn of the early 1880s materialised, Dresser & Holme may well have been financially

(Footnote 57:   A copy of the prospectus is in the Dorman Museum, Middlesbrough.)

(Footnote 58:   This is evident from the Linthorpe prospectus.)

(Footnote 59:   This is explicit in the Art Furnisher's Alliance reference to the Tees Bottling Company in their 1880 prospectus.)

(Footnote 60:   *The Furniture Gazette* 23 August 1879.)

(Footnote 61:   I have some unease about the dates of Dresser finishing with Hukin & Heath, and starting with Dixon but the evidence for late 1879 seems convincing.)

(Footnote 62:   *The Furniture Gazette* 13 November 1880, p 304.)

(Footnote 63:   Mrs Beesley, formerly of the Sutton Local Studies Centre tells me that Dresser's name appears in the Sutton Rates Book in September 1882 for Wellesley Lodge. Stanley, his youngest boy, started at the Whitgift School, Croydon in 1883, and the three youngest girls at Sutton High School, in 1884.)

over exposed. This early recession brought down many firms including the well-known furniture makers and furnishers Jackson & Graham in May 1882 with debts of £215,000 [64] and a year later the Art Furnisher's Alliance.

On 8 July 1882, a short announcement appeared in the *The Furniture Gazette* [65] announcing the dissolution of the partnership between Dresser and Holme, with Holme shouldering the debts (and credits) of the company. Dresser, it was announced would henceforth *"devote the whole of his time to his professional work as an architect and ornamentist."*

fig 18   Water Jug by Perry Son & Co. c.1885.   Cat. M-079

1882-1904

When Dresser moved to Wellesley Lodge, Sutton in 1882, he was 48 years old. He was still young enough to pick up the pieces of his life, and this is exactly what he did. His contracts with Dixon and the Art Furnishers Alliance were still in force, and these are only two about which we know. The status of his studio in Sutton seems to have been something about which we can only guess. Whether his staff removed also to Sutton, or whether he recruited anew is also unknown. It would appear that Wellesley Lodge was not large enough to house the Dresser family and studio. The house had three reception rooms, and ten bedrooms of which five were described as "very small." [66] The house had a market value of £3,300 (in 1902), and was leased to Dresser from 1882 to circa 1889. The first reference to Dresser's Sutton studio was in 1884 when he rented a small house in Carshalton Road, Sutton as a studio.[67] By 1886, Dresser had moved his studio to Brunswick Road, Sutton.[68] It was not until 1889, when Dresser moved to Barnes, that the Studio was re-located with the family. The studio was on the top floor of his house, Elmbank, where it stayed until his death in 1904.[69]

Meanwhile, the Art Furnisher's Alliance, though it made an operating profit, was unable to cover its overall liabilities. The Alliance persevered until Spring 1883, and Dresser seems to have retained an active participation. In July 1882,[70] *The Furniture Gazette* notes an exhibition to promote cheap wall decoration. Dresser had always shown a distaste for white walls and white ceilings in that they 'killed' other decoration in the room. Under the heading 'Cheap Decoration,' *The Furniture Gazette* reported:

> *"...A novel exhibition, ... consisting of a series of examples of wall decoration, produced by the exclusive use of ordinary brown paper, sugar paper, soap paper, and other cheap materials...... (shows that) ..true art effects can by these means, be harmoniously introduced..."*

Although this exhibition seems to have been unreported elsewhere, this is exactly the sort of innovation at which Dresser excelled. It is doubtful if such innovation would have appealed to the upper class residents of nearby Mayfair, but it was an idea that might inspire the many people unable to afford the expensive wallpapers of Jeffreys, or William Morris and Co. Such use of brown paper, ironically, was to become fashionable in the 1960s in many 'trendy' shops, being suitable for display purposes as the perfect neutral background.

During 1883, Dresser suffered the agony of the Art Furnishers Alliance being declared bankrupt. This was the last of the great creative ventures to promote 'good taste' in which he was involved. The backers of the Alliance were unwilling to give more time and money to the operation, and eventually two furniture makers involved with Chubb & Co. applied to the courts for a bankruptcy order. This is perhaps the nadir of Dresser's fortunes.

With the close of 1883, matters seemed to improve and stabilise. Dresser's friend, Arthur Liberty, a fellow shareholder in the Alliance, seems to have offered some help. Dresser designed textiles for Liberty, according to Barbara Morris, as early as 1882, and during the mid and late 1880s, many of Dresser's designs became established favourites at Liberty, such as the Kordofan candlestick, registered in 1883 by R. Perry Son & Co. of Wolverhampton and the four-leg 'Thebes' stool. A version of the Thebes stool was sold by the Art Furnishers' Alliance and later by Liberty. Perry was a supplier to Liberty and the Yuletide catalogue published by Liberty in 1890, shows not only the Kordofan candlestick but other Perry items. In 1888, Liberty also launched the Clutha range of glass made by James Couper & Co. of Glasgow. There is also the suggestion that Dresser may have designed the Norfolk range of furniture for Liberty (Liberty's answer to the Morris Sussex range?). That there was a close relationship between Dresser and Liberty, I have little doubt, but hard evidence is scarce. Both Liberty and Dresser were close friends with Charles Holme and Liberty probably had trade dealings with Dresser & Holme. Furthermore, Dresser's son, Louis Leo, found employment at Liberty in 1896, the year of his marriage.[71]

1884 was a more positive year for Dresser. Elkington produced several Dresser designs. The Old Hall Earthenware Co. also seems to have negotiated a contract. Sadly, however, neither of these two companies reached the heights of innovation shown in the designs of Hukin & Heath and Dixon. Old Hall did not use the innovative shapes or glazes used by Linthorpe. Both preferred to use safer shapes and safer decoration. While both companies produced unmistakably Dresser designs, they might well have been produced in Dresser's pre-1877 period.

Dresser, however, seems to have found more sympathy from the cheaper end of the metalware trade. R. Perry, Wolverhampton probably negotiated a contract with Dresser around 1883, and a glance at fig 18 shows the new innovative Dresser coming once again to the fore, as do many of the designs that are attributable to Benham and Froud during this period.

Work seems to have been plentiful. In early 1884, he is recorded apologising to the Architectural Association for his failure to prepare a lecture as he had been called away unexpectedly to visit ten cities in the previous week. Dresser's Studio is re-established in its own right, and in 1886, Dresser found time to produce *Modern Ornamentation,* a collection of designs suitable for home furnishings. It is Dresser's last known publication, but added little in the way of innovative designs and applications to those which are apparent in *Studies in Design,* 1874.

In 1888, Dresser embarked on one of his last great innovative ventures, that with Liberty for Clutha glass. The Clutha name was registered under the name of Arthur Liberty and was marketed by Liberty's store. Manufactured by James Couper & Sons, Glasgow, it was the realisation of many of Dresser's dreams about glass,

(Footnote 64:   *The Furniture Gazette* 20 May 1882.)
(Footnote 65:   *The Furniture Gazette* 8 July 1882 p.26.)
(Footnote 66:   PRO; IR58 81009. From a description made in 1902, by the Inland Revenue.)
(Footnote 67:   *Kelly's Directory.*)
(Footnote 68:   I am indebted to Maureen Beesley, formerly of Sutton Archives for information on Dresser's Sutton addresses.)
(Footnote 69:   1891 Census returns.)
(Footnote 70:   *The Furniture Gazette* 22 July 1882.)
(Footnote 71:   Liberty Staff magazine, *The Lamplighter.*)

fig 19

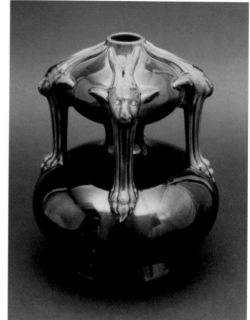

fig 20

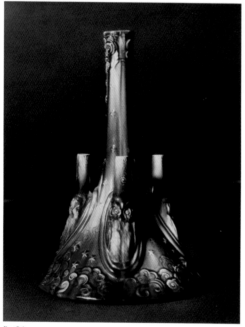

fig 21

fig 22

figs 19 & 22 Vases attributed to Dresser and Ault. *Courtesy of D. Bonsall*
fig 20 Ault Goats Head vase by Dresser. Cat. C-131
fig 21 Ault vases attributed to Dresser. *Private Collection*

and the principles about which he wrote in his earlier books. Clutha glass is innovative in the same way as Hukin & Heath, Linthorpe, and Dixon. Some forms are organic, some are a re-run of his ceramic shapes and some are reminiscent of earlier civilisations, but the best of Dresser's identified Clutha designs all show his distinctive touch.

In 1889, Dresser, when he moved from Sutton to Barnes took a lease on a substantial house overlooking the Thames. The house was demolished circa 1906, and no description of the layout exists. We do know, however, from the Richmond Rates books that it was the largest house in the immediate area, and that it had large gardens and stables. The 1891 census return shows that there was a live-in maid employed as a 'studio-maid.'

A second maid was listed as 'Parlour Maid Downstairs,' seemingly Mrs Dresser drew a distinguishing line between domestic and work establishments. It is also interesting that Dresser, in the 1891 census, simply described himself as a "designer of Art Patterns for Manufacture" as compared with his 1881 entry as "ornamentist and merchant".

It appears from Stuart Durant's account of his interview with Frederick Burrows that Dresser was happy to spend his time either gardening, or travelling to sell his studio's designs. His studio seems to have been a stable operation and there were good relationships between the master and staff. Most of the studio work seems to have been for textiles and wallpapers, including Anaglypta. However, there was to be one more notable venture with William Ault in 1893. In his work for Ault, we see Dresser taking his interpretation of the grotesque in a very individual direction. Dresser's work in the 1860s often carried grotesque elements, but somehow with Ault a new dimension emerged, viz., the 'Tongues,' 'Chinese Masks' and 'Goats Head' vases. If one is also prepared to credit Dresser with some of Ault's unsigned shapes, see figs. 19, 21 & 22, we are left wondering about the inspirational sources he used. It has been suggested to me that the tongues' vase may represent ectoplasm. It is an area of research that I have been wary of pursuing. However, Dresser was extremely well-read and may have used motifs associated with the supernatural, without necessarily believing in such doctrines.

Apart from the occasional mention of Dresser in the early 1890s, one of which included a reference to a lamp with the "human form as a handle" [72] he receives increasingly less coverage in the trade press. He may by then have been seen as 'yesterday's man' and the favourable article on him by Charles Holme in *The Studio* in 1898 [73] is indeed a retrospect, with no promise of exciting new ventures. The textiles which are featured showing Art Nouveau, Beardsley and Voysey-like patterns are presumably from the Dresser studio, rather than by Dresser himself.

As the Durant-Burrows interview suggests, Dresser was content to keep a genial eye on matters, while spending an increasing time on his flowers and social pursuits. He seemed to remain genial to the last.

Dresser's last journey was to Mulhouse in eastern France [74] in company with his son, Louis Leo. Mulhouse was the manufacturing base for Jean Zuber. Dresser died of a heart attack there in November, 1904, and was buried in an unmarked grave.

The obituaries of Dresser duly recorded the highlights of his career but none have explained Dresser better than the article in *The Studio* by his friend Charles Holme in 1898. Dresser, Holmes said, was prepared to embrace industry, and someone like Dresser should not be spurned by the purists of the Arts & Crafts Movement on the grounds that he was profit-motivated rather than creating solely for art's sake.

> "Mr (sic) *Dresser is in a way the figurehead of the professional as opposed to the quasi-amateur designer* .... [75]

> .... "*There is a danger lest the work of many a good ally may be forgotten if the cuckoo cry that Morris was not only the greatest, but the only leader of the movement is left without occasional protest.*[76]

> "*The strenuous efforts of Mr (sic) Dresser to raise the national level of design, not by producing costly bric-a-brac for millionaires, but by dealing with products within the reach of the middle classes, if not the masses themselves, deserve very hearty recognition.*" [77]

(Footnote 72:   *Cabinet Maker* 1 October 1888, p.103 "*...lamps.. Several very quaint examples with human figures for handles were shown to us from the pencil of Dr. Dresser...*")

(Footnote 73:   *The Studio* Vol. XV, p 104 Although unsigned, I have little doubt that the article is by the Editor, his old friend and business partner, Charles Holme.)

(Footnote 74:   Then Mulhausen in Germany.)

(Footnote 75:   *The Studio* Vol. XV, p.106.)

(Footnote 76:   Ibid. p.108.)

(Footnote 77:   Ibid. p.110.)

Wallpaper

Dresser's ideal for inside wallcoverings was as 'background.' In *Ornamental Art,* 1862, p.43, Dresser drew an analogy with walking towards a clump of trees. In the distance, trees are blobs of colour, but only as one approaches, may the detail manifest itself.

Consequently, Dresser's wallpaper is not meant to overpower and grab attention as the first thing to be noticed on entering a room. This is the reason why the design of Dresser's 1867 Gemini paper specially re-produced for this exhibition is in 'small case'. Bigger would be vulgar, unless the scale of the room was also increased. On entering a room decorated with Dresser wallpaper, the first observation of the paper should be as a colour harmony giving background to the people and the furniture. Afterwards, one may examine the paper closer and then discern the mastery of the design.

This is something Dresser would have learned from Owen Jones, whose 1850's designs for Townsend, Parker, Townsend are in the Sanderson archives. I understand from an interior designer formerly working in the Palace of Westminster, that it is also a recurring problem with designers at Westminster to keep the scale of Pugin's wallpapers in proportion to the rooms.

fig 23   *The Ipswich Sketch Book, p.52.*
Courtesy of Ipswich Borough Council

This short article cannot do justice to Dresser's work in wallpaper. More time and research is needed to justify his position as a major influence on the development of wallpaper. Indeed, there is little that Dresser wrote on wall decoration in his time which is not as relevant today as it was then.

The Building News in 1865 cites Dresser as well-known for his wallpapers and carpets. An exhibition in Liverpool in the same year featured Dresser's papers. A scan through the wallpaper registrations for the 1860s at the PODR suggests William Cooke of Leeds as a producer of Dresser designs.[78] *The Ipswich Sketch Book* q.v. and fig.23, shows an envelope dated 1864 from John Allan of Bow. The wallpaper, Gemini, is from the Jeffrey workbooks, circa 1867. Dresser also served as a juror on the paper-hangings panel at the Paris International Exhibition, 1878.

In spite of Dresser's credentials in wallpaper design, he seemed to prefer painted walls with 'powderings' using stencils. He wrote about the lack of hygiene in the use of wall coverings, as a haven for vermin. Moreover, the evidence of Dresser's surviving interior decorations support Dresser's preference for stencilling rather than papering. Once again, it is not difficult to see the influence of Owen Jones, famous for the months he spent in Spain absorbing the decoration and ornamental schemes at the Alhambra Palace.

Dresser maintained an active interest in paper design throughout his career, though it is likely that many of the later designs, including some of those in *The Studio* article of November 1898, are from the Dresser studio rather than Dresser himself. Dresser also designed Anaglypta papers for Lincrusta Walton. These designs were still being run in the 1900s.

Dresser's hey-day in paper design must be in the 1870s. Towards the end of this decade, he was distracted by his other projects at a time when the floral and more classical designs of Crane, Day, and Morris were in the ascendancy. Dresser seems to have lost his supremacy.

Firms for whom Dresser designed are: John Allan, London; Scott Cuthbertson, London; William Cooke, Leeds; Jeffrey & Co., London; William Woollams & Co., London; Lightbown, Aspinall & Co., Pendleton; Sanderson & Sons, London; John Line; Lincrusta, Walton, Sunbury.

fig 24   Wallpaper designed by Dresser for Steiner & Co., Manchester and reproduced in *The Studio* article on Dresser, November 1898. This paper was discovered in a bathroom believed to have been decorated in the 1960s and thought to be contemporary. The 1960s manufacturer is not known. *Courtesy of Isobel Carew-Cox*

(Footnote 78:   Cooke was also a shareholder in the Art Furnisher's Alliance.)

Artwork in the Minton archive.
Courtesy of Royal Doulton, plc

fig 26

Ceramics

Dresser designed ceramics throughout his working life. The evidence establishes dates between 1851, when he won a prize at the School of Design, through until 1896 when his contract with Ault finished. His first customer seems to have been Minton prior to the London International Exhibition in 1862. He also designed for Wedgwood, Watcombe (q.v.) Old Hall, Linthorpe and Ault. Among other firms Dresser may have designed for, are Brownfield, and Brown Westhead Moore, on stylistic evidence. Also likely is Royal Worcester, but the experts on Worcester reject this claim on the grounds that Worcester had no need of outside designers. The above names are some of the more obvious contenders which may have purchased one-off designs from Dresser. Moreover, the fact that Dresser was invited to become a member of the ceramics jury at the Philadelphia Centennial Exhibition, 1876 [79] suggests an international dimension to his ceramics involvement. I have tried to find evidence for Theodore Deck and Dresser working in design collaboration, but have failed to establish any. Nevertheless, it is tantalising that Londos promoted Deck's work for the opening of a new warehouse in 1876, at the same time as Dresser was the Londos Art Director.[80] A Villeroy and Boch link is also unproven, but see Cat. C-206 to C-208.

Dresser's principles on the form and decoration of ceramics are laid down in his published works. He respected the plasticity of clay in producing a traditional thrown shape, but this did not prevent him from accepting and designing moulded ceramics. It was more important to Dresser that beautiful ceramics were affordable using industrial techniques rather than dwelling on expensive labour-intensive craft methods.

Dresser's most productive period for ceramics was during his Linthorpe contract, 1879-1882 when he was Art Director. He was then in a position to implement his ideas and avoid the excesses of 'mix and match' - an inevitable consequence to which his designs were subjected, once he sold his designs and placed them in the hands of staff designers.

Dresser's designs for Ault in the first phase of his contract, also exhibit his ideas in an unadulterated form, and show a new side to his designs by using human and animal forms, albeit in a stylised way.

As in so many other spheres of Dresser's work there is much of universal and timeless truth in what he writes on ceramics. It may be an instruction to decorate only the rim of a dinner plate, or the positioning of a handle on a jug, but much of his work could have been written today.

fig 25, left   Detail of Minton Vase at fig 29. *Private Collection*

(Footnote 79:   *The Furniture Gazette* 6 May 1876. Dresser declined the invitation.)
(Footnote 80:   *The Furniture Gazette* 1876. I have also failed to establish any link with either Sarreguemines or Massier.)

A · MOONLIGHT · SCENE ·

THE · ORIGINAL · ETIHOPIAN · SERENADERS ·

fig 27   Artwork in the Minton archives.   *Courtesy of Royal Doulton, plc*

Minton

It is accepted that Dresser designed for Minton at the 1862 exhibition [81] although the hard proof is non-existent. However, it is likely that Dresser's involvement was earlier, via the School of Design, or Owen Jones and included tiles.

The Ipswich Sketch Book shows shapes and decoration which can be linked to Minton. However, the most prolific source for Dresser's work at Minton is the *Art Director's Work Book,* which has a probable date of 1871. This book is thought to have been collated at a time when the Art Pottery Studio was established in Kensington, and using patterns then in production. There are 22 entries some of which cover more than one design. The entries have been satisfactorily matched to designs in the Minton archives, and they comprise a valuable source reference to Dresser's work.

It is quite probable that a number of these designs pre-date 1871, such as the border designs used on dinner plates. Equally there is no reference in the *Art Director's Work Book* to the vase a detail of which is shown at fig 28, exhibited at Paris in 1867, suggesting that the decoration for this vase was not in current production.

Cloisonné designs are much more difficult. There is a presumption currently, that if an article is Minton cloisonné, it is Dresser. This is highly unlikely. cloisonné made an impact when exhibited at London, 1871, but several examples appear earlier, (see fig 31) where the left hand vase has an 1868 datemark. Many of the designs on Minton cloisonné look very un-Dresserlike, some have ribbons and bows. From examples in the antiques market, most cloisonné seem to be dated post 1871, and the decoration is a mix of Dresser-like elements with other standard decoration. Pure Dresser decoration tends to come in the earlier pieces i.e. pre-1872 (see Joan Jones, *Minton,* Annex 'A' for year dating.) I have seen little evidence for any association between Minton and Dresser in new designs produced after 1871.

fig 28, right   Detail from a vase made for the 1867 Paris exhibition.
Courtesy of Nicolaus Boston Antiques

(Footnote 81:   Joan Jones, *Minton.*)

fig 29, top   Minton. *(left to right)* 'Beetle Vase' ;10"; year mark 1872. Vase; 5.8" other marks indistinct. Flower Holder; 6.5", shape 1494. Other marks indistinct. *Private Collection*

fig 30, left   Artwork from the Minton archives. *Courtesy of Royal Doulton, plc.* (This vase is sketched in *The Ipswich Sketch Book,* p.3)

fig 31, above Minton. Cat. C-153 and C-154. Dated 1868 and c.1870 respectively

fig 32, right   Detail of Minton vase. Year mark 1873. *Private Collection*

Wedgwood

There is no doubt that Dresser produced designs for Wedgwood in the period 1866-1868. A Wedgwood plate with a Dresser border was photographed by Pevsner in possession of the Dresser daughters. This artwork for the border is preserved, titled 'Dresser border,' in the Wedgwood archive, see fig 35. It was also used as decoration on vases, and several different colour ways are given in the work books.

Other examples of Dresser's work are shown here and overleaf. Examples are infrequent, and decoration tends to be of the 'spiky' variety. I am not aware of much other information on Wedgwood and Dresser, but available evidence suggests a short relationship around the period 1866-1869. Designs were registered in the PODR during 1867.

*fig 35   Wedgwood plate with 'Dresser Border'.
Courtesy of The Getty Research Institute*

fig 33, left   Minton Vase.   *Private Collection*

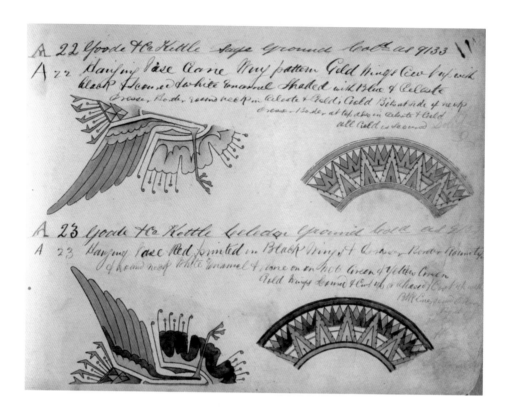

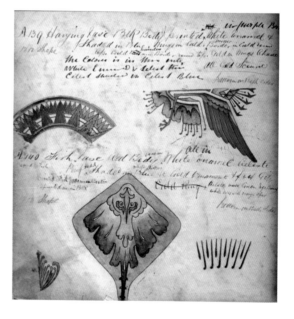

fig 36, top, fig 37, left, fig 38, above Artwork in The Wedgwood Archive. *By Courtesy of The Trustees of The Wedgwood Museum, Barlaston, Stoke-on-Trent, Staffordshire*
fig 39, right Wedgwood Vase. *Private Collection*

fig 40   Vase impressed 'Watcombe Torquay' and '188'.
Courtesy of Andrew McIntosh Patrick

Watcombe Pottery

I have seen no documentary evidence that connects Dresser and Watcombe pottery. However, the stylistic evidence is so strong that I have little doubt in classifying Watcombe pots as 'B' in the grading used in the selling section of this catalogue. Some with a less strong affinity, have been categorised 'C'. Sadly, the Watcombe Pottery records no longer exist.

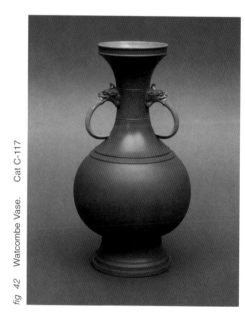

Watcombe Pottery started the manufacture of art pottery in 1867, in a small way [82] in Torquay, Devon. Many of the early Watcombe pots reflect Japanese inspiration, which would have suited Dresser's thinking. The vase at fig 42 is a good example of the early style, and compares closely with fig 106 in Dresser's *Principles,* 1873.

The surface decoration in much of the early Watcombe also reflects Dresser. One decoration using the flying crane, is very similar to that in the Minton archive which bears Dresser's signature. A further example, quoted by Laurence Rogers in his booklet on Watcombe is the decorative motif at fig 182 *Principles* which has been identified on Watcombe pots and a plate.

fig 41   Watcombe Vase. Private Collection

fig 42   Watcombe Vase.   Cat C-117

Other stylistic similarities between Watcombe and Dresser exist. One such can be seen at fig 44. The design of the terracotta jug was registered at the PODR by Watcombe in 1872. This basic shape is illustrated at figs. 45 & 46 which is signed by Dresser, fig 47.

One other piece of evidence has been cited by Michael Whiteway of Haslam & Whiteway. Charles Handley Read, a well-known and respected collector, reported he had at last obtained some evidence of Dresser's work for Watcombe. Unfortunately, Handley-Read died before citing the evidence. From his knowledge of Handley-Read, Michael Whiteway believes some credence should be given to the report.

In sum, the stylistic evidence is strong, and has been accepted since the renaissance of Dresser in the 1970s. One other aspect of the evidence for a connection is rather less certain viz., Dresser's gift to the Emperor of Japan in January 1877. It is sometimes cited in support of the Watcombe-Dresser connection that the Dresser gift contained examples of Watcombe and therefore one might assume Dresser had chosen some of his own work. However, the available evidence from Tokyo contains only one disappointing piece of Watcombe, a plate with a possible Dresser border, and a centre of a sweetly pretty bird perched on a branch. More evidence may be forthcoming, since many ceramic items have still not been traced.

It is perhaps wiser to rely on the stylistic evidence of a Dresser-Watcombe connection. Even to a purist, reluctant to ascribe a connection without formal evidence, it must surely be agreed that such Watcombe is worth collecting in its own right. It shows a strong Dresser influence, and to that extent, are good examples of Dresser's style.

fig 44, left to right   Four Jugs, Clutha glass, Watcombe terracotta, Unidentified metal, Watcombe terracotta.
Courtesy of D. Bonsall

(Footnote 82:   *Christopher Dresser and the Torquay Pottery* by Laurence Rogers.)

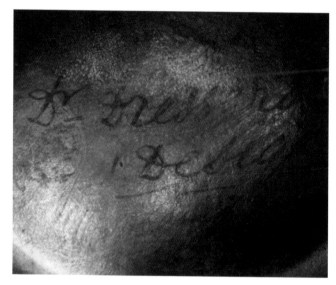

fig 45, top Two metal Jugs by Fearncombe. Three terracotta Jugs by Watcombe. *L to R* Cat. M-083, C-104, M-084, C-113, C-108.
fig 46, left Jug, no manufacturers mark. *Private Collection*
fig 47, above Signature on base of fig 46.
This jug was bought in Portobello Market in the 1970's and has been in a private collection ever since. It is believed to be authentic.

fig 48   Linthorpe. Unglazed, shape 586.   Courtesy of D. Bonsall

Linthorpe Pottery

Introduction

Linthorpe Pottery can justifiably lay claim to coming closest to Dresser's ideal for pottery. It broadly satisfied Dresser's wish for affordability and good design. It also showed Dresser's wisdom in selecting Henry Tooth to run the pottery and create the glaze effects.

If asked for a quick 'sound-bite' about Linthorpe, I think it would have to be *'shape and glaze effects.'* Linthorpe stunned the Victorian consumer, and as an antiques dealer carrying a fair range of Linthorpe, I can verify that it still stuns many a customer today.

An appreciation of Linthorpe requires each piece to be examined on its own merits, for some pieces have survived the firing process better than others. Some are overfired and overglazed, often obliterating the incised decoration. A good example, however, where the random effects of firing have excelled on a satisfying shape is something to rejoice over.

History

Linthorpe Pottery was the first phase of an 'art manufactures' complex at Middlesbrough in Northern England. The funding was provided by John Harrison, a general entrepreneur, but the impetus came from Christopher Dresser, following a visit to Teesside probably some time around late 1874. Dresser reputedly was moved by the plight of the Teesside unemployed, and suggested the manufacture of pottery using the local beds of brick clay. This would probably have pleased Dresser in another way, in that he delighted in pointing out that beautiful objects can be

fig 49 Linthorpe Vases and three 'Propeller' Vases by Ault. *Private Collection*

made from the basest of materials. Presumably, Dresser's workload and his Japanese pre-occupation intervened until his return from Japan in June 1877. One can assume that on his return, contact between Dresser and Harrison was resumed and an agreement to proceed was reached. The first pots were produced in early 1879 (I have actually seen one dated 7-2-79), so if one projects backwards, we can assume that agreement was reached in late 1877.

Dresser would have suggested Henry Tooth as manager of the enterprise. It would have been a very bold step to appoint him, if the enterprise was only to be concerned with pottery, for Tooth had no experience in pottery. This makes it more likely that the idea of an art complex, producing wallpaper and glass in addition to pottery was intended, as was stated in the 'offer for shares' published early 1879. Dresser presumably took the view that an artist can be taught the skills of running a pottery, a glass factory, and a wall-paper manufactory, whereas a factory manager cannot necessarily be taught the skills of an artist.

Henry Tooth was packed off to learn the skills of pottery and its glazes in 1878, and spent a period of months with T.G. Green at Church Gresley, South Derbyshire.[83] Having finished his apprenticeship, he set up the pottery with technical help recruited both in Middlesbrough and elsewhere.

fig 50 Linthorpe Vases. *Private Collection*

fig 51   Linthorpe selection.   Private Collection

Dresser provided designs, and all ware leaving the pottery carried his 'facsimile' signature. Tooth felt competent to start production at around mid-1879. The first pots appeared on display in Middlesbrough in Autumn 1879, where the local people were amazed at what could be produced from 'local muck'. Shortly afterwards, a display was mounted in Dresser & Holme's new London warehouse, in November 1879.

> *"The wares of Linthorpe are as yet, of three kinds. First, there is an undecorated ware, which pretends to pleasant forms and welcome colours. Second ... a ware enriched with boldly incised ornament* (and some) *perforated. Third ... pieces which are enriched with bold painting in enamel colours of flowers and birds."* [84]

During 1880, Dresser & Holme as the pottery's agents promoted Linthorpe with advertisements in *The Pottery Gazette*. Several influential customers supported the pottery, including the Art Furnishers' Alliance, and Chubb & Co.[85]

During 1881, Dresser provided further designs for Linthorpe, such as those photographed by Pevsner from Dresser's account book. These designs appear to be for shapes, suitable for moulding. Not many of these have been identified, and the pot shown at fig 55 is an exception. It is interesting and carries a high shape number, 2119, which is well beyond the normal Dresser range of numbers.

Little is known about events in 1881, but it is apparent that John Harrison, the owner and promoter of Linthorpe was disappointed at the progress of the Linthorpe venture. The ceramics venture succeeded, but nothing came of the promised wallpaper and glass ventures. One also assumes that the impetus of the pottery success was faltering. Dresser was obviously pre-occupied with the growing problems of the Art Furnishers Alliance, his health and impending financial problems. Whatever the reasons, Harrison took over the promotion and sale of Linthorpe from Dresser & Holme with effect from January 1882. Also at this time, Dresser seems to have vacated his post as Art Superintendent, followed later by Henry Tooth who left to form his own pottery at Church Gresley, South Derbyshire, in partnership with one William Ault.

(Footnote 83:   This company still exists and is perhaps more famous for its Cornish range of kitchenware)
(Footnote 84:   *The Pottery Gazette* Dec 1879. p 476.)
(Footnote 85:   Chubb had several pieces of Linthorpe when they auctioned off the contents of their redundant saleroom near St. Pauls in May 1882.)

fig 52

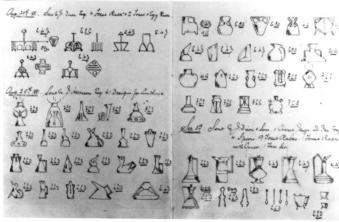

fig 53

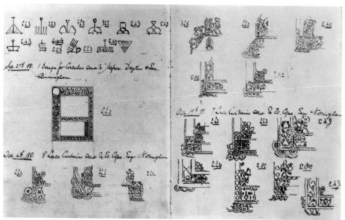

fig 54

figs 52, 53, 54   Photographs taken for Nikolaus Pevsner in 1936

Thereafter, Linthorpe carried on until 1889, when the pottery closed with the death of John Harrison. The product of Linthorpe became more 'Victorian' in taste after Dresser's departure, producing more traditional shapes, usually with floral decoration. Many Dresser favourites continued in production, but without the presence of Tooth or the influence of Dresser, the product degraded thereby losing impact. In 1890, a break-up sale of Linthorpe pottery took place. This included the moulds which were largely bought by William Ault, and the Torquay Terracotta Company for its subsidiary, Stapleton. Both companies produced from these moulds, and the Stapleton moulds were re-run in the late 1920s under the name Daison.

On collecting Linthorpe, Dresser enthusiasts will invariably look for a shape number under 1,000. The highest number recording a Dresser facsimile is 928, which is recorded by Clive Hart in his book on Linthorpe.[86] Some of the most exciting Dresser shapes appear in the 3xx band, and the numbers are usually hand incised, otherwise the numbers are stamped.

However, I believe that after Dresser cut his connection with Linthorpe, his facsimile as a guarantee of 'good art qualities' was no longer used. I suspect that several designs of Dresser would have been in the pipeline at the time, and many of these would have been produced in later years. Such an example is Shape 2119 at fig.55 mentioned above. Shape 2119 bears a high number, a late Linthorpe mark and no facsimile. Not all such Dresser-like designs can be so verified. Therefore, if one is buying a Linthorpe pot with a shape number higher than 928, there is an element of 'at your own risk.'

(Footnote 86:   Hart also records the number 1700 but this is thought to be a rogue number or mistake.)

fig 55   Linthorpe Jug. Shape 2119. Unsigned, but see the design in Dresser's note book, fig 53, which is sketched on the second line of the Linthorpe entries for August 29th 1881. The existence of this jug with a late mark and a high number illustrates the point that many Dresser designs were run after Dresser cut his Linthorpe connection.   Cat. C-082

fig 58   Old Hall Porcelain.   Cat. C-172

Old Hall Earthenware,
Old Hall Porcelain

Most examples of Old Hall are earthenware.The company produced a range of porcelain however, in 1886, during which time it was producing Dresser designs. There is no documentary evidence of Dresser's association with Old Hall, but the fact of his facsimile signature appearing on many pieces, leaves no room for doubting the association. The earliest date for Dresser's designs would appear to be late 1884. Registrations for some of the Old Hall shapes used for Dresser decoration appear at this time. Other shapes associated with Dresser were registered in 1886 - see figs. 59 & 60. It is these shapes which carry the Dresser facsimile, suggesting a contract at this time, similar to that for Ault (q.v.). The example at fig 58 is in porcelain and presumably is close to the 1886 date at which Old Hall introduced the porcelain range.

The decoration on Old Hall appears to be a good example of how decoration degraded as time went by. The colourways were changed gradually, until the whole presentation simply lost its colour sense and cohesion.

The shapes for table services show some originality with the employment of a shallow depression in the rim of a dinner plate to hold condiments. Likewise, the extra depression in the base of a soup plate to facilitate the scooping up of the last of its contents.

fig 56, above left   Old Hall c.1886.   Note the use of stylised human form.   *Private Collection*
fig 57, below left   Old Hall c.1886.   *Private Collection*

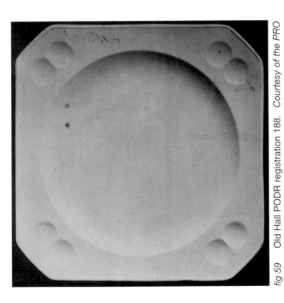

fig 59   Old Hall PODR registration 188.   *Courtesy of the PRO*

fig 60   Eureka pattern. See Cat. C-193.   *Courtesy of the PRO*

Ault

William Ault had an early connection with Dresser through his partnership with Henry Tooth in 1883 when they formed Tooth & Ault. In 1887, Tooth and Ault went their separate ways with Ault leaving to form a new pottery.

On the collapse of Linthorpe, Ault bought several moulds from the break-up sale in 1890. These would include shape numbers 128, 138, 177 and 189, which are identified Linthorpe shapes.

In 1891, it is understood that Ault made payments to Dresser, according to a letter to the V&A in 1952 from the then owner of the pottery, but it is likely that this represented payment for 'one-off' designs and they are not identified.

In 1893, however, Dresser signed an exclusive contract with William Ault, whereby he committed himself to provide designs for Ault to the exclusion of other potters. This contract is reproduced on the following page. It is an important document, which may be an exemplar for the exclusive type of contract that Dresser signed with other companies. It also reflects Dresser's claim that his services could be acquired for the cost of a staff designer. This contract also reflects Dresser's concern that he should monitor the quality of Ault's output bearing his facsimile signature, following the lessons he learned with other potteries such as Old Hall.

The shapes produced under this contract bearing the Dresser facsimile which have so far been identified run from shape No. 216 to No. 323. As with Linthorpe it is likely that Dresser designs were produced after the finish of the contract, bearing higher numbers but without the facsimile.

It has been suggested to me that it would be worthwhile exploring Dresser's link with the supernatural shown in some Ault shapes. One theory being that the 'tongues' vase shows ectoplasm rather than elongated tongues (fig.65). The pots shown at figs 19 21 & 22 are also raised in discussion. I believe that if there is anything in this suggestion, it is likely that it reflects the fact that Dresser was very well read and au fait with most lines of thought. I raise it as others may wish to explore further.

Ault Dresser contract:

Note. The original is written in italic script, and is difficult to read. Clauses 6-9 of the contract have been left out.

An agreement made the thirty first day of May - One Thousand eight hundred and ninety three BETWEEN Christopher Dresser of Elm Bank, Barnes in the County of Surrey architect and art designer of the one part and William Ault of Swadlincote in the County of Derby, Pottery manufacturer of the other part whereby it is mutually agreed as follows:

1. The said Christopher Dresser shall from time to time design patterns for objects to be wrought in clay for the said William Ault and the said Christopher Dresser shall not during the continuance of the agreement design fancy objects to be made in clay for any other potter.

2. This agreement shall continue in force for the term of three years to be computed from the twenty-fifth day of March One thousand eight hundred and ninety three determinable nevertheless in manner hereinafter appearing.

3. The said William Ault shall during the continuance of this agreement pay to the said Christopher Dresser the sums following that is to say - in the first year of the said term, the sum of one hundred pounds. For the second year of the said term the sum of Two hundred pounds. And for the third year of the said term, the sum of three hundred pounds. The said sums respectively shall be paid by the said William Ault to the said Christopher Dresser by four equal quarterly instalments on the twenty fifth day of March, the twenty fourth day of June, the twenty ninth day of September and the twenty fifth day of December in each year. and the first quarterly instalment of the said sum of One hundred pounds shall be paid by the said William Ault to the said Christopher Dresser on the twenty fourth day of June one thousand eight hundred and ninety three.

4. The said Christopher Dresser shall if requested by the said William Ault visit the pottery of the said William Ault twice in each year during the continuance of this Agreement for the purpose of inspecting the production of objects from the patterns of him the said Christopher Dresser and the said Christopher Dresser shall instruct the workmen of the said William Ault and criticise objects already made and the said William Ault shall pay to the said Christopher Dresser upon each visit his travelling expenses to and from Swadlincote, from and to London first class and one guinea a day for a period not exceeding three days on the occasion of each visit for hotel expenses.

5. The said William Ault shall during the continuance of this agreement stamp or cause to be stamped on all objects made from the designs of the said Christopher Dresser in legible characters, the words 'Dr Dresser' and the said William Ault shall not during the continuance of the Agreement stamp the said words or permit the name to be stamped on any object which shall not have been designed by the said Christopher Dresser.

As witness the hands of the said parties

C Dresser

Signed by Christopher Dresser in the presence of

Edwin H Jeffrey
150 Hurlingham Road
Fulham S.W.

fig 64   Ault Vase, facsimile Christopher Dresser. Shape 322. Cat. C-142

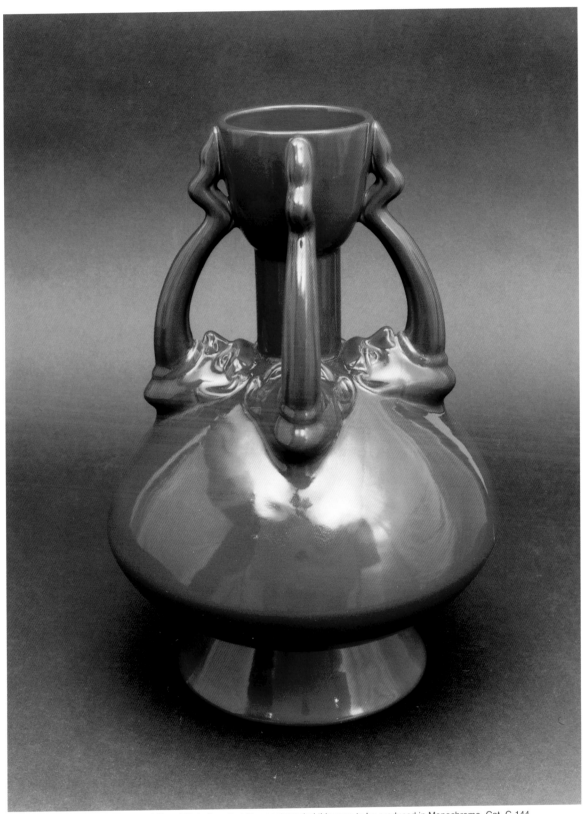

fig 65   Ault 'Tongues' Vase. We believe that Dresser intended this vase to be produced in Monochrome. Cat. C-144

fig 66   Benham & Froud copper and brass Ewer. 12"/30cm.   *Private Collection*

fig 67   Elkington plated Pots c.1885. The classic Bowl on the right was sketched in *The Ipswich Sketch Book* c.1865. The shape no. 247 suggests it may have been taken from *The Elkington Silver Book.*   *Courtesy of D. Bonsall*

Metalware

Metalware, undoubtedly attracts the highest prices for Dresser. A bid of £115,000 (hammer) was paid at Bukowski's Auction Rooms in Stockholm in April 1998 for a Dixon tea-pot of which other examples were known to exist. Many Dresser dealers were shocked but were to be even more shocked when a selling exhibition of Dresser in New York in November 1998 sold well over half its exhibits; some prices approaching the Bukowski sale-price. Clearly, if Dresser is as good as his promoters believe in producing designs that were ahead of their time - then Dresser is an essential name to promote in any collection covering design in the 19th and 20th centuries. Unfortunately, the pool of available examples of good Dresser metalware is insufficient to go round.

The attraction of Dresser's metalwork lies in its simplicity, and the pre-Modernist appearance of his post 1876 designs. Dresser designed metalwork well before 1876, (see fig 74) but it is after 1876 that his confidence and inventiveness are given full reign. In August 1879, a 'ground-breaking' exhibition of metalware was held to inaugurate Hukin & Heath's new London showrooms. This is described in the section on Hukin & Heath (q.v.) and it started a momentum for a fundamental change away from the 'wedding-cake' productions previously used. A report by *The Furniture Gazette* [87] refers to the geometry of the exhibits, and epithets such as 'absurdly simple', 'hexagonal plan', 'rhomboidal opening' are used in descriptions. Most importantly,

> *"Many of these articles are designed with an express view of bringing really good and artistic metal-work within the reach of those who cannot afford to invest in expensive and intricate work; they are (mostly) of a severe design, their beauty consisting rather in their outline than in the amount of labour bestowed on their manufacture."*

(Footnote 87:   *The Furniture Gazette.* 23 August 1879.)

'Form follows function' is a slogan which has been hi-jacked by the Bauhaus/Modernist movements. Yet throughout the 19th century, reformers championed this philosophy. Horatio Greenough, an American, published his ideas on art and architecture in 1852 and 1853 well before Frank Lloyd Wright.[88] The first reference to buildings which 'may be called machines' came from Greenough in the early 1850s, not Le Corbusier.[89] The School of Design at South Kensington taught 'Form follows function' throughout the 1850s and Dresser wrote about 'form follows function' in his *Technical Educator* articles in 1872.

Dresser was the first designer in any meaningful lasting way, to put the doctrine of 'Form follows function' into actual practice, and it was something he tried to achieve throughout his design career.

Is it not ironic that Pevsner wrote his article on Dresser in 1937, as the result of researching the origins of the Modernist Movement. Pevsner discovered two cruet sets during his research on Modernism and discovered they bore Dresser's name. As a result of this the article in *The Architectural Review* was published.

Another attraction in Dresser's metalware is that he designed for companies which produced good craftsmanship. Most Dresser metalware has a high content of hand-finishing. In the case of the two companies, Dixon and Perry, work associated with Dresser is of a consistently higher standard than their normal range.

As in all other fields of Dresser's designs, metalware degraded in purity of form and restraint, the further they were removed from his involvement. Nowhere, is this more apparent than with Hukin & Heath when it produced adaptations of Dresser's designs. Many of these adaptations were produced in the 1890s in silver, bearing the Heath and Middleton marks. It is important to make this point, because some high prices have been paid for such metalware, including £5,200 (hammer) for an elongated Heath and Middleton claret jug at Christies, London in November 1998. I do not believe that Dresser designed this elongated shape, nor would he have approved of it. It makes an absolute mockery of his writings on the placing of handles and spouts in his *Technical Educator* articles. The Heath & Middleton hallmark was registered in 1884, some four years after Dresser ceased his connection and all Heath and Middleton pieces must be viewed with this in mind. Having said which, many Heath & Middleton pieces are very eye-catching and stand as good pieces in their own right, but few are Dresser.

A. Kenrick & Sons, Birmingham

This is a recent identification and research is ongoing.

fig 68, *above left*   Examples of Doorstops and one Fire Iron Rest by A. Kenrick and Sons.   *Private Collection*
fig 69, *below left*   Coalbrookdale Doorstop and three Fire Iron Rests c.1872.   *Private Collection*

(Footnote 88:   *The Travels, Observations. and Experience of a Yankee Stonecutter* New York 1852 and *Memorial of Horatio Greenough* New York 1853.)

(Footnote 89:   Greenough's essay on American Architecture printed in *The Memorial* op.cit.)

fig 70   Hukin & Heath Tray, c.1880. Cat. M-042.
Elkington Tea Service, 1882. Cat. M-004.
Note the Sugar Bowl is sketched in *The Ipswich Sketch Book*, fig 93

16594.   R.ᵈ 22869.

4 gills 10/.

6 gills com/.

1/3 scale round

March 11ᵗʰ 1885.   Dresser.

fig 71   Elkington Sketch Book. See Cat. M-002.
Courtesy of V&A Museum

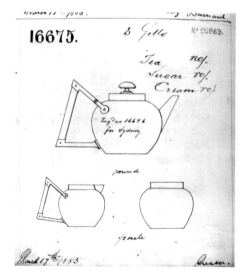

16675.   3 Gills   R.ᵈ 22863.

Tea 70/.
Sugar 70/.
Cream 70/.

Reg. no 16646
for Sydney

round

1/3 scale

March 17ᵗʰ 1885

fig 72   Elkington Sketch Book.
Courtesy of V&A Museum

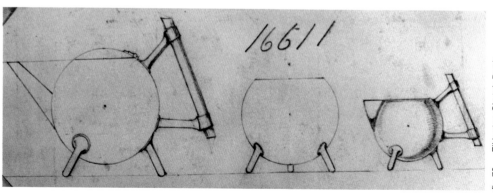

16611

fig 73   Elkington Sketch Book.
Courtesy of Birmingham City Arcives

fig 74   Elkington Salt Cellar, 1872.   Cat. M-007

Elkington & Co. Birmingham

Elkington is probably the metalware company with which Dresser had his longest association. Dresser was designing for Elkington in the 1860s.

> *"...Messrs Elkington have long had in preparation a class of goods for* (ornamental) *purposes, from designs by Dr. Christopher Dresser and which .... will come between the costly beaten work and the meretricious common ware.... accustomed to adorn the tables of our middle classes at many a suburban villa .... A collection of these will probably be sent to the Paris Exhibition in 1867."* (*Building News* 29 December 1865).

Elkington may not have produced the designs mentioned above, the phrase 'long had in preparation' seems ominous, perhaps shapes such as that at fig.70 were too avant garde for a company over-used to manufacturing heavily decorated ware. The appearance of similar shapes in *The Ipswich Sketch Book* leaves little room for doubt that Dresser had these shapes in mind in the mid-1860s. In the event, the example at fig 74 bears the year mark for 1873 and shows that Elkington may have run some Dresser designs, rather gingerly. The example at fig 70 has the mark for 1882, and one might assume that it was the success of Hukin & Heath and Dixon that spurred Elkington into producing, somewhat belatedly, Dresser's designs.

In 1885, Elkington started to register the more avant-garde designs by Dresser with the PODR. This did not however exclude production of some older Gothic designs which may have been sold by Dresser in the 1860s. If this supposition is correct, it may go some way to explaining the otherwise bizarre system of numbering shapes covering a range from 247 to 18,655.

Elkington is one of the few companies on which there is some evidence of payment scales for designers. A letter to Pevsner from the company in 1950 [90] gives selected detail. Predictably, there were 'very few details' on Dresser's payments, and none were quoted in the letter.

It is perhaps significant that Dresser's name is not marked on any Elkington pieces, this may have been company policy, but just as likely it may have been the absence of any formal contract between Dresser and Elkington such as we see from the Ault contract. (q.v.)

(Footnote 90:   *Pevsner archive, The Getty Centre.* The letter says Morel Ladeuil agreed a five-year contract at £400 per year, though in the latter years he seems to have drawn £1,500 per annum. The staff designer, Willms, started at £600 per annum in 1868 rising to £700 in 1873.)

Coalbrookdale, Shropshire

Dresser designed for Coalbrookdale in the late 1860s. Identified designs appear in PODR records in 1867, immediately before the Paris exhibition. Registrations, with a Dresser connotation continue through until the early 1870s. Dresser's best known designs for Coalbrookdale are for coat and umbrella stands, but some doorstops and fire-iron rests bear his style. Dresser claimed he designed park gates for a large estate. It would also be surprising if Dresser had not also designed street railings, balcony rails and fire-surrounds.

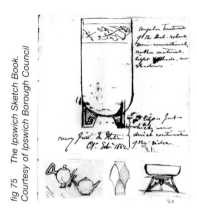

fig 75 The Ipswich Sketch Book. Courtesy of Ipswich Borough Council

fig 76 R. Hodd Jug. See handles in fig 75. Cat. M-001

Richard Hodd and Son, London

It is likely that Hodd executed Dresser designs. The jug, fig 76, stamped with a Hodd mark used between 1872 and 1881 carries the same handle, as a sketch shown in *The Ipswich Sketch Book,* fig 75.

Between 1878 and 1881, Dresser is thought to have had an exclusive contract with Hukin and Heath, and then Dixon. Consequently, it is likely that Hodd executed the designs before 1878. I have seen no documentary evidence for an association, the evidence is stylistic.

fig 77 Spheres and Feet. Benham & Froud Kettle, Cat. M-086. Webb Glass. Dixon Biscuit Barrel, Cat. M-061. Minton Bowl, Cat. C-156

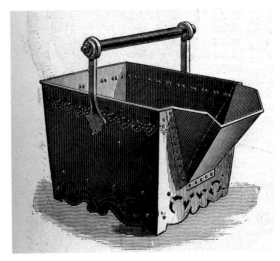

fig 78   'The Sutton' *The Cabinet Maker* 1886.
Note the absence of a metal liner

Benham & Froud, London

Dresser's association with Benham & Froud started as early as 1871 when he designed wooden coal boxes for the company (See Furniture Section). Dresser's metalwork is mostly dated to the 1880s or 1890s, but metal designs would have been produced in the 1870s. Dresser designed coal-boxes with metal fixtures throughout the period, so why not metalware per se.[91]

No Dresser signatures appear on Benham & Froud metalware, so it is probable that Dresser produced occasional designs rather than under a contract. We can be certain about the kettle at fig 77, below left, as Pevsner photographed it in the Dresser daughter's household, and the coal scuttle at fig 78 named 'The Sutton.' Other items must be deduced on stylistic grounds.

Halen in his book promotes mixed metalware.[92] Plaques using this process are to be seen on some coal-boxes. The metal process was patented in 1885, by the staff designer R.W. Laws, which is a reasonable date for Dresser to have been involved. However, one must be careful of attributing all mixed metal designs to Dresser.

There are two other areas, where Dresser is thought to have designed for Benham & Froud, viz., lighting and hammered-iron ware.

Lighting

In October 1888, *The Cabinet Maker* reports;

> "... *Lamps in all forms and sizes are produced* (by Benham & Froud). *Several very quaint examples, with human figures for handles, were shown to us from the pencil of Dr. Dresser* ..." [93]

No Dresser lighting by Benham & Froud has been identified, let alone examples in the above quote. Presumably, the human handles received a treatment similar to that in fig 56.

(Footnote 91:   *The Furniture Gazette* 1876 and *The Cabinet Maker* 1889.)

(Footnote 92:   See Halen *Christopher Dresser,* fig 192.)

(Footnote 93:   *The Cabinet Maker* 1 October 1888 p.103.)

Hammered Iron

In June 1882, the Art Furnishers Alliance held an exhibition of hammered iron work.

> "The productions of the new art are from the designs of Dr. Dresser, FLS. A spray of a daisy enclosed in its leaves - all perfectly formed by the hammer - is what people have been accustomed to see only in silver. Chandeliers, gaseliers and candelabra of exquisite designs are also on view .... They neither discolour or rust, as boiled oil is used in the manufacture of the metal. Ornamented, but still practical, kettles, iron frames for screens, balconies for windows, door plates, hinges and scroll work with Wedgwood medallions in the centre, show to what a variety of uses, hammered iron can be put..." (The Cabinet Maker, July 1882 p.4)

Who made the iron described above? It could have been imported by Dresser & Holme, but I believe Benham & Froud is a much more likely candidate. In an article on an exhibition in 1894, twelve years later, a reference is made to;

> "...the strides which have been made in the development of wrought iron since its revival in this country... has grown to play an important part in the business of the house furnisher ..." (The Cabinet Maker, May 1894)

It is perhaps significant that at least two of the prize-winners at the above exhibition were employees of Benham & Froud.

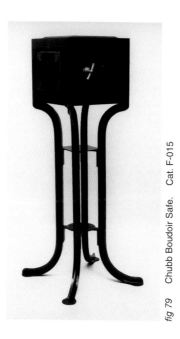

fig 79   Chubb Boudoir Safe.   Cat. F-015

Chubb & Sons: Wolverhampton and London

Dresser was presumably involved with Chubbs before the Art Furnishers Alliance in 1881. During the late 1870s, Chubbs produced a range of ecclesiastical ornaments, such as chalices, and a range of Spanish medieval door furniture. Dresser was interested in Spanish metalware and sent an assistant to Spain and Morocco to research the subject.[94] During his art editorship of The Furniture Gazette, Dresser published some of Chubb's designs. It is assumed these designs were adapted by Dresser. Such examples were used in Bushloe House.

The boudoir safe at fig 79 is usually attributed to Dresser, but there is no documentary evidence. However, there seems to be no reason why Dresser should not have been involved in Chubb's main manufactures.

fig 80　An Indian Pot, Hukin & Heath. The shape number 1831 is close to the Dresser range, suggesting it was chosen by Dresser for reproduction in England.　Cat. M-054

Hukin & Heath: Birmingham

The date of Dresser's association with Hukin & Heath is uncertain, perhaps late 1877. In 1879, Dresser is described as 'Art Advisor' to the company.[95]

This description is confirmed by *The Furniture Gazette;*

> *"the firm have secured the services* (of Dr Dresser) *in order to be reliable in point of design"* (*The Furniture Gazette 23* August 1879)

I believe that metalware produced by Hukin & Heath which carries the stamp "Designed by Dr Dresser" means just that, but other ware produced at the time was merely approved by Dresser, as being in accordance with good design and would not be so marked. Dresser would have had an exclusive contract with Hukin & Heath, on the lines of that with Ault (q.v.). Thus, not all shapes produced 1877-79 were Dresser designs.

fig 81　Ipswich Sketch Book.　Courtesy of Ipswich Borough Council.　See entries for Cat. M-029, and C-159

In August 1879, Hukin & Heath opened new premises at 19 Charterhouse Street, around the corner from Dresser & Holme's warehouse. The occasion was used to launch a new image of Hukin and Heath. The rooms were decorated to set out the new products. A report by *The Furniture Gazette,*[96] and one may assume that Dresser would have prompted the reporter, makes it clear that this is a new departure:

> *"No more wedding-cake art, the rapid strides that have been made ... in ornamentation* (including) *furniture... decoration of walls, ceilings and floors, have at last overtaken the precious metals".*

Dresser is obviously publicising the fact that his attempts to produce new metal designs are at last bearing fruit. *The Furniture Gazette* article is important to those who wish to understand Dresser's metalware, for I believe that the Hukin & Heath exhibition marks a watershed in the development of metalware for household use.

(Footnote 94:　*The Furniture Gazette,* 2 May 1874, p. 426.)

(Footnote 95:　*The Architects Journal,* 1879, p.222.)

(Footnote 96:　*The Furniture Gazette,* 23 August 1879 p.124.)

fig 82   Hukin & Heath Claret Jug. Dresser mark.   Cat. M-034

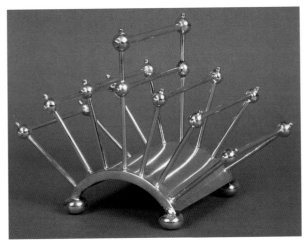

fig 83   Toast Rack. PODR mark 1881.   Cat. M-030

The reaction of the three to four hundred visitors who attended the private preview was positive. A momentum for change was created and carried through via Dixon and Elkington to Perry and Benham & Froud. Indeed, if I read the evidence correctly, it gave Elkington (q.v.) the confidence to run some of the designs which Dresser had earlier submitted, (see fig 70.)

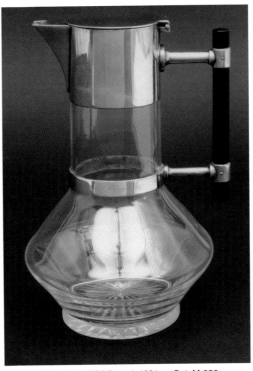

fig 84   Claret Jug. PODR mark 1881.   Cat. M-036

As Art Advisor, rather than merely a supplier of designs, Dresser was presumably responsible for extending Hukin & Heath's interests to include items of Indian and Japanese origin. Anticipating modern sourcing of manufacture and materials, as happens with twentieth century multi-nationals, Hukin & Heath ran an operation in both Persia and the Indian sub-continent to produce 'works-of-art' which on occasion were copied and produced for UK manufacture, (see fig 80.)

The Hukin & Heath exhibition also showed items of Japanese design, which were copied and manufactured in the UK. The report, unfortunately, does not identify the items. Therefore it is not possible to assess the shape numbers which would enable us to distinguish articles made during Dresser's contract, and later examples by staff designers produced to meet the aesthetic craze. A quote by *The Art Journal* may best describe the Persian and Japanese items:

> *"Messrs Hukin & Heath reproduce several of the Persian and Japanese Art Works with accuracy unsurpassed - perfect copies indeed - by the electric process: such specimens, being selected for reproduction by Dr. Dresser, are of course, always beautiful examples of Art."* (The Art Journal 1879 p.222)

It is not known when Dresser left Hukin & Heath, but his designs appear in the Dixon workbook marked 1879. This would leave little time between the Hukin & Heath exhibition in August and a new Dixon contract with shapes appearing in the 1879 workbooks. For working purposes, I assume that the August 1879, exhibition is Dresser's last work for Hukin & Heath.

The illustrations of Hukin & Heath's metalware needs no explanation which is not covered by *The Furniture Gazette* article. Several designs were produced after 1879 which are attributed to Dresser. Registrations of the toast/letter racks and the claret jugs (see figs 83 & 84) are both dated May 1881, and neither has ever been noted with a Dresser acknowledgement. It is easy to see a Dresser influence and consequently, an attribution has been made in the catalogue entry. If a Dresser contract existed, then there would have been no necessity to use the Dresser mark after August 1879.

Hukin & Heath were creditors of the Art Furnishers Alliance, in 1883, which may suggest that Dresser's relationships with the company were not totally strained.

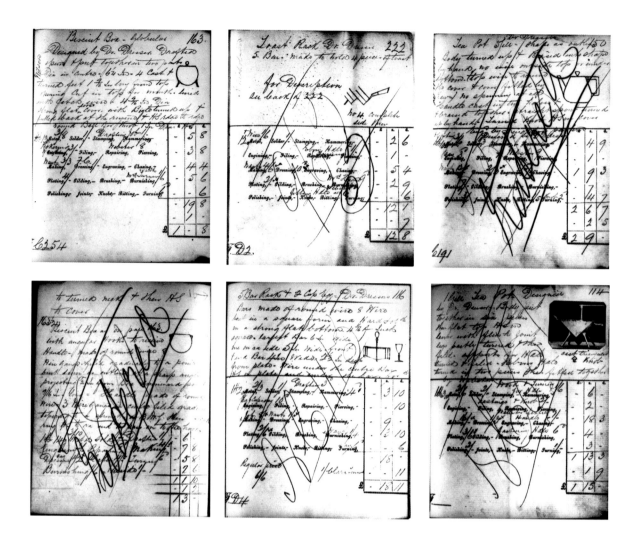

figs 85, 86, 87, 88, 89 & 90.   *Dixon Workbooks.*   See Cat. M-061, M-062, M-066.
Courtesy of Head of Leisure Services, Sheffield

J. Dixon & Sons: Sheffield

The earliest indication of Dresser's work for Dixon is the inclusion of six very exotic tea-pots in the 1879 workbook. As explained in the Hukin & Heath section this is an unexpectedly early date for the start of any formal contract between Dresser & Dixon. The contract may have run for some three years. Designs appear in the workbooks from late 1879 to early 1883, with a concentration around the year 1881, which reflects Dresser's own account book (See figs 85 to 90).

Information on Dixon is sparse. There is little reference to the company in contemporary periodicals. Nevertheless, the examples shown in this catalogue, speak eloquently. More so, than Hukin & Heath, Dixon carried through Dresser's work to show some very simple, stylish shapes, decades ahead of their time. There are no references to imaginative promotions such as with Hukin & Heath. By this stage Dresser was stretched with his commitments to the Art Furnishers Alliance, Dresser & Holme, and the publication of *'Japan',* not to mention illness. Consequently, this most imaginative period of Dresser's work is left with the shortest account.

fig 91   The Kordofan Candlestick.   Courtesy of Isobel Carew-Cox

Richard Perry Son & Co. Wolverhampton

Perry, like Dixon, produced some of the best and most innovative designs, and like Dixon, there is little information. The earliest record of Dresser's association with Perry is the 1883 registration of the Kordofan candlestick which carries a Dresser label (See fig 91) The Kordofan and other Perry items appear in Liberty catalogues around 1890, and it is plausible that Dresser arranged sales with Liberty. Perry's main business was as a japanner, and thus would have come to Dresser's notice. The quality of Perry's work may not have reached the standards of other metalware manufacturers, but the quality of Perry items linked to Dresser is of a better quality than most other Perry items. This may indicate Dresser's close involvement. I have seen no japanned pieces, as such, which may be linked to Dresser, but Liberty sold Perry items in 'art colours,' using a not dissimilar process to japanning.

fig 92   Perry Barnstick c.1885.   Courtesy of D. Bonsall

fig 93   The Ipswich Sketch Book.
Courtesy of Ipswich Borough Council

The Ipswich Sketch Book

The Ipswich Sketch Book, believed to be Dresser's own sketch book was bought at auction in 1972, by the Ipswich Museum, where it is presently held. The previous history is unknown. I cannot see any reason to doubt its authenticity. Many sketches have been done in pencil, and there is some fading. By and large, it is well preserved, apart from a few doodles by a bored child in the pre-1972 period. The integrity of the designs, however, is not compromised.

Quasi-Inspiration

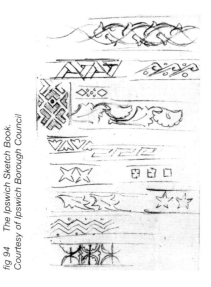

fig 94   The Ipswich Sketch Book.
Courtesy of Ipswich Borough Council

"Quasi-inspiration" is a term used by Dresser to describe the phases of intense creativity which arise very occasionally in an artist's life. Dresser went out of his way to disclaim that this was in any sense related to taking 'unnatural substances,' but he was at a loss to explain the phenomenon. Dresser originally wrote a chapter for his book *Principles* to be published in the *Technical Educator,* 1872, but had second thoughts. The chapter was later published in the journal, *The Warehouseman* in 1875, using the phrase "quasi-inspiration".

In "quasi-Inspiration," Dresser describes a sort of dreamy aura which surrounded him one golden sunny Autumn evening. An urge to sketch suddenly seized him, and the designs which resulted bore no relation to any that he had done before. On a second occasion in the early-mid 1860s, another powerful aura [97] descended, which lingered on for some 24 hours. Dresser ran out of sketching paper, and he seized envelopes and the backs of photographs to serve as an alternative.

The Ipswich Sketch Book, contains several mounted scraps of paper, and a few envelope backs, see figs 23 and 93, 94 & 95. It seems reasonable to relate Dresser's quasi-inspiration to these sketches. Many of the sketches in *The Ipswich Sketch Book* contain ornamentation which is uniquely Dresser, and when one sees this applied to objects in the round, it is instantly recognisable.

Dresser was extremely well-read and aware. He would have heard about the effects of laudanum and its followers in English Society. Indeed he could have heard stories from Owen Jones' extensive travels. Romantic as it might otherwise be, I see no reason to doubt Dresser's explicit denials of a drug-related inspiration, and take the phenomenon at face value.

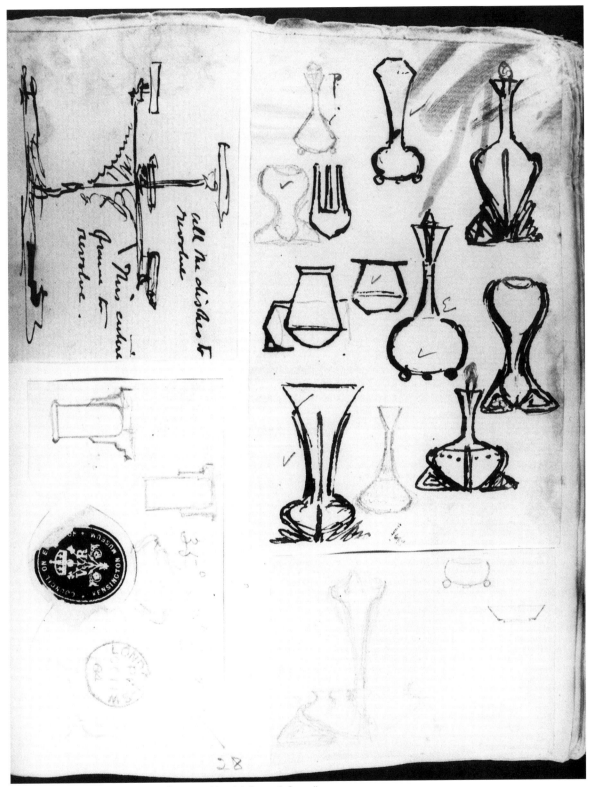

fig 95   The Ipswich Sketch Book.   Courtesy of Ipswich Borough Council

(Footnote 97:   My phrase not Dresser's.)

JAPAN

The Dresser gift to
His Imperial Majesty the Emperor of Japan,
26 January 1877

The origin and impetus for this gift came in mid-1876 from Philip Cunliffe Owen, then Director of the South Kensington Museum. Dresser had decided to make a trip round the world to include the Philadelphia Centennial Exhibition, 1876, Japan and China. The latter two places were outposts of the Oriental importing firm Londos based in London where he was employed as Art Advisor.

Hearing of Dresser's plans, Cunliffe Owen suggested that Dresser escort a gift of European art manufactures to present to the National Museum in Tokyo. This gift was intended as a goodwill gesture to replace a lost consignment of 'art manufactures' bought by the Japanese in Vienna in 1873 as exemplars for their emergent industry. Accordingly, Londos co-ordinated a package and 'friends' were asked to 'ante' up. Most of the donations came from those with whom Dresser would have had business contacts. Presumably Cunliffe Owen's prestige was also used, Elkington for example who manufactured electrotype replicas of the South Kensington Museum's holdings. The detail can only, however, be surmised.

Dresser set sail from Liverpool for New York in October 1876, and arrived in Japan on Boxing Day 1876, via Philadelphia. At Philadelphia, Dresser met General Saigo, the head of the Japanese delegation to the Exhibition. The two men obviously hit it off and they sailed together from San Francisco to Yokohama. On arrival, Dresser was treated as an honoured guest, and received considerable hospitality and favours. Dresser reported to the British Embassy to make arrangements for handing over the donation to the Museum. Presumably due to General Saigo's influence the Emperor agreed to accept the donation on behalf of the Museum. In return, the Emperor decreed that Dresser was to be an honoured guest, given unprecedented access to the Imperial treasures, and given an escort to travel more or less as he pleased to inspect Japanese working and manufacturing practices.

The rest of the story and an account of Dresser's travels in Japan are in his book *Japan* published in 1882. However, one would assume that the Emperor's unexpected generosity had an effect on Dresser's travel plans. This would account for Dresser's fleeting visit to Canton, where Londos had an office. It was presumably more productive to avail himself of the Emperor's generosity. I would guess that perhaps Londos itself did not share Dresser's enthusiasm, and this may well explain the absence of references to Londos after Dresser's travels.

Why, for example, did Dresser not use Londos to exhibit an example of a Japanese roof sent to him by the Emperor and exhibited at Streeter's of Bond Street in 1878? Maybe if Londos had paid all or part of the costs for the visit, there would have been grounds for complaint.

The Gift

It is the contents of the gift itself that are of major interest to students of Dresser. The gift was intended for the National Museum, Tokyo, and indeed Dresser spent some time explaining and arranging the exhibits to go on show. Not all of the exhibits have been identified. The first serious effort seems to have been in 1990, when Pearsons plc, owner of both Minton and Doulton tried to identify their component of the gift. Many of these were identified, and some appear in *Minton* by Joan Jones. However, by persistence and the generous help and the time of two Japanese friends, Takeshi Furuya and Keiji Suzuki, a carpet, some glass and a piece of Watcombe, have recently come to light.

fig 97 Watcombe Plate donated to Japan, 1876.
Courtesy of The National Museum, Tokyo

There are two problems that confronted identification. Firstly, the role of the National Museum. Its area of interest ends in the 1850s, before the opening up of Japan. This explains why the gift was put into store, rather than researched. Secondly, the first effort to translate ended up like a game of Chinese whispers. Dresser's English was translated into court Japanese, then into modern Japanese and back into English. After three translations, it was not surprising that several re-translations were confusing. Here Keiji Suzuki appeared. With legendary efficiency Keiji, together with the National Museum ran down the original material and we learned for example that 'Fat Compton Mill Pottery' was indeed 'Watcombe terracotta' and Yves Boutrel was a piece of Doulton decorated by F. Butler.

fig 98 Minton Plate donated to Japan, 1876.
Courtesy of The National Museum, Tokyo

The gift itself comprised 315 items, of which over 50 have been identified. The Museum classified the gift into the following categories:

Pictures - 81, (donated by the South Kensington Museum); Textiles - 32; Paper - 2; Ceramics and glass - 182; Lacquer - 6; Sculpture - 12 (I assume that these are Elkington 'Museum' replicas)

It is interesting that more ceramics have been identified than in other categories. Perhaps this reflects the impetus of Pearson plc research together with Mr Ito the ceramics and glass curator. Detailed research in other categories of the gift may reveal further identifications. It will be interesting to learn what was catalogued as 'lacquer' and 'sculpture'.

The early days of research into this gift were motivated by the assumption that Dresser would have favoured items of his own design over other items. This has not proved to be the case. The Wedgwood vases, for example, are classical Jasperware and not Dresser's work. Further, the Watcombe plate pictured at fig 97 does not recommend itself as Dresser's work, and does little to prove the link between Dresser and Watcombe. Some Minton plates, however, are identified as Dresser and indeed one is pictured both at fig.98 and Cat. C-146. Identified glass has not, however, yet proved anything either way, because we are not sure what glass Dresser was designing before 1876. This must be an area for further research.

An area which has not been researched is a second gift by Dresser in 1878, taken out to Japan by his son, Christopher. This gift consisted of 1,201 items. An initial scan of the list suggests that the figure of 1,201 is not as grand as it seems. It may be for example that a box of different wools was catalogued as several items rather than one. Further research is needed to clarify this. Moreover, if Dresser paid for and selected the items brought out by his son, it may well contain a higher proportion of items designed or associated with Dresser. The items are annotated "donated by Christopher Dresser" and not by Londos, Dresser & Holme, nor any manufacturer. Frustratingly, with four months to go at the time of writing, I will not have any answers before exhibiting.

Hopefully, these are areas that may be researched fully before the Exhibition by the Metropolitan Museum, New York in 2002, and hopefully by our own V&A Museum in 2004, the centenary of Dresser's death.

Textiles

The plates on this page are from PODR records for the early 1870s. The brilliance of colour is well brought out by the use of silk and wool. J.C. Ward, Halifax, figs 101 & 102 is documented as a manufacturer of Dresser designs. It is suggested that Holdsworth, Halifax, figs 99 & 100 also manufactured Dresser designs.

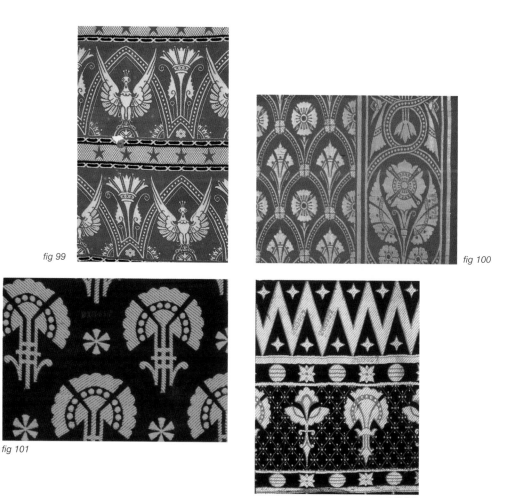

fig 99

fig 100

fig 101

fig 102

figs 99, 100, PODR Registrations by Holdsworth, 1872/73
figs 101, 102 PODR Registrations by J.C. Ward, Halifax. *Courtesy of The PRO*

fig 103 Textile. Cat.T-007

Carpets

Like wallpaper, carpets are not intended, other than as a background in a room. One's eye is not meant to be drawn to a carpet on entering a room. It is an area of harmonious colour, which when inspected at close range will reveal a pleasing pattern. Carpets should be 'bloomy' i.e. resembling the flowers in the grass of a common when out strolling. 'Bloomy' meant small areas of bright or primary colour.

The Building News mentioned Dresser in 1865 as "well-known" for his carpet designs. The first specific reference I have seen to Dresser and carpets is in G.A. Sala's book on the Paris Exhibition 1867. It is not difficult to see Dresser's theories coming out in Sala's account. These carpets were designed for and exhibited by Brinton & Lewis, Kidderminster.

In 1869, John Lewis left Brinton & Lewis, and moved to Halifax to join his uncles at Crossleys. Dresser would appear to have followed Lewis. Dresser not only designed carpets for Crossley, some of which were exhibited at the London Exhibition, 1871, but also designed the layout and decoration of many rooms in the company's headquarters including the studio of the Design team. Dresser seems to have had an exclusive term contract with Crossley (see fig 16). In 1871, John Lewis left Crossleys to run his own carpet manufactory. Dresser designed for the short-lived operation, some four years, of this manufactory. Lewis exhibited at Vienna in 1873 but it seems he disappointed Dresser by not producing all-silk carpets to rival those exhibited by the Austrian company, Haas.

In 1876, Dresser wrote the section on carpets for George Bevan's *British Manufacturing Industries,* a detailed handbook for anyone wishing to understand carpets, their design requirements, and manufacturing processes at this time.

In 1878, Dresser is recorded as designing for Brinton, who exhibited his designs at the Paris Exhibition that year. Thereafter, I have seen little evidence of Dresser designing carpets except for the carpets illustrated in *Modern Ornamentation,* 1886. Nellie Dresser, a daughter who entered the Dresser studio in 1889 was unable to recall any examples of carpet manufacture in her attachment which lasted up to 1904.

fig 104   Carpet by John Lewis, Halifax c.1876, donated to Japan, 1876.   *Courtesy of The National Museum, Tokyo*

fig 105 The reverse side of the carpet at fig 104.
Courtesy of The National Museum, Tokyo

Dresser's theories on carpet designs were quoted by F.J. Mayers in 1934 [98] as relevant in 1934, as they were in Dresser's own time.

> "...Some three quarters of a century back, Dr Christopher Dresser, a designer of much initiative and ability, lectured on sanity and fitness in design... Many manufacturers bought his designs freely and produced them, and although many of them were really excellent designs, they were mostly failures commercially. They were probably above the heads of the purchasing public... But Dresser's principles of design hold good today and need but the most trifling revisions to make them adoptable as guides for the development of design in the present and the future. THERE IS NOTHING WHATEVER THAT OUR ART TEACHERS ARE NOW PREACHING THAT HE DID NOT SAY SIXTY OR SEVENTY YEARS AGO..." (The upper case in this quotation is mine.)

The above quote is from a recognised authority on carpets. Mayers started his apprenticeship circa 1880 in a designer's studio, but he never identified it. This was a time when Dresser was at the height of his authority, and his theories would have been known and discussed. On p.130 of his book, he summarises Dresser's theory as;

> "Dresser's idea of a background is 'neutrality' of colour, either via tertiary tones or by a close mingling of richer colours to produce a natural 'glow'. His ideal background evidently was the effect one gets in a Feraghan carpet, with a small version of the Herati design, a rich mixture of strong colours in very small masses as a dark ground..."

On page 123, Mayers added that Dresser believed a carpet should be seen satisfactorily from any point of view, and commented (p.107) that this was something that Voysey, for example, did not understand. Voysey often designed carpets the pattern of which could only be viewed correctly from one position, as in wallpaper and fabric designs. This is something Dresser was always careful to avoid.

In this exhibition are some fragments of a carpet that were once in Allangate, Halifax, (Cat. T-001) and at fig 104 is a photograph of a carpet brought to Japan by Dresser in 1876, from John Lewis of Halifax.

I am aware of three companies for whom Dresser designed. These are Brinton & Lewis (later Brinton), Kidderminster, Crossley, Halifax and John Lewis, Halifax.

According to F.J. Mayers in a quote above, "many manufacturers" bought Dresser designs. One might speculate that this included Templeton of Glasgow, for whom Owen Jones designed. As Mayer was working during Dresser's lifetime, and researching at a time when many from the 1860s and 1870s, were still alive. I would credit his description of "many manufacturers." This would suggest that Dresser also designed for European and American manufacturers. We know that in 1873 after the Vienna Exhibition, the US Government invited Dresser to report on the American Carpet Industry which was then in the same dire state that the British found themselves twenty years earlier. There must be more information about this report and its consequences available to a determined researcher.

(Footnote 98: *Carpet Designs and Designing,* 1934, F.J. Mayers)

fig 107 Clutha Vases c.1888.
Courtesy of D. Bonsall.

GLASS

by Christopher Morley

Dated between 1861-65, *The Ipswich Sketch Book* contains several references to glass including 'opaque glass' 'opaque crackled' and 'dogstooth cut to feet' (see figs 93, & 95). In 1865, Dresser lectured on the decoration of glass [99] to the Society for the Encouragement of Fine Arts on glass and crockeryware. In 1871, Dresser claimed 'there was not a branch of art manufacture for which he did not regularly design patterns.' [100] In 1873, eight pages in *Principles* refer to glass specifically, illustrating 28 shapes. Clutha glass was introduced in 1888, and has remained the only 'proven' Dresser glass. Why the delay?

It seems hardly credible that Dresser should have waited until 1888, before launching his glass designs, which in the case of Clutha is as revolutionary as his better known metalwork, and possibly more influential. Is it not more likely that, in view of his early writings on glass, he designed in this field throughout his career? Sale prices of minimalist metalwork by Dresser confirm amongst other things, what the marketplace values most highly in Dresser's work. But it seems unlikely that earlier Dresser glass would mimic his metalwork designs.

Conversely Linthorpe remains modestly priced, except for the most unusual examples, and perhaps this is a reflection of the lack of appreciation of this aspect of Dresser's work. Yet, bearing in mind the plastic nature of both pottery and glass as Dresser did,[101] Linthorpe might well be the vital clue as to what other glass by Dresser might have looked like at a similar date. The impact of much of Dresser's work for Minton and Wedgwood at an even earlier date is achieved not so much from form and glaze as is largely the case with Linthorpe, but more from applied decoration. This also may be taken as a clue to help identify another phase of Dresser's glass.

Dresser singled out Phillipe Brocard's enamelled glass for praise at the Vienna Exhibition, 1873. It is intriguing that Dresser should also have exhibited Brocard's glass at his Art City Warehouse exhibition in 1876. According to *The Furniture Gazette* reporter, Dresser even bought up the entire UK allocation of Brocard's glass. No documentary evidence exists, but a design link would not be surprising.

It ought to be stated clearly at this point that Clutha remains the only fully authenticated Dresser glass, apart from the remarkable windows at Allangate, Halifax and Bushloe House, Leicester. All other glass discussed here is presented as prompts to further research.

What remains to be said of Clutha Glass that hasn't been said already?

fig 106, left   Clutha vase, 's' profiled lip c.1888.   Cat. G-011

(Footnote 99:   *The Builder* 25 March 1865, page 215.)

(Footnote 100:   *Ornamentation considered as High Art. RSA Journal* 1871.)

(Footnote 101:   *Principles* 1873.)

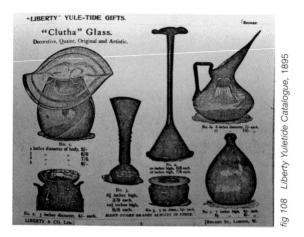

fig 108   Liberty Yuletide Catalogue, 1895

Cosmic Clutha

Clutha was introduced in 1888.[102] Various dates have been published previously but without verification, strange as it might seem, considering this aspect of Dresser's work was written up as early as 1937.[103] 1888 is perhaps a later date than expected, but the correspondence between James Couper and Sons and *The Pottery Gazette*, about an infringement of Clutha designs by Webb's Roman glass, together with the registration by Liberty of his Clutha mark, provides proof beyond reasonable doubt of this date.[104]

No further correspondence on Webb's infringement has been noted and no example of Webb's Old Roman has yet been identified. Presumably some agreement was achieved. It is somewhat ironic that the following year, at the Paris 1889 exhibition, Clutha glass is displayed in the joint Goode, Webb and Copeland pavilion, in our illustration of which Webb's name is most prominent (see fig 112).

The subject of wholesale and retail sales in this period is most complex, as is apparent from Couper's reference to "our Clutha glass" which they had restricted to Messrs Liberty, at that stage, and for which they registered their own mark on 20 February 1889, shortly before the Paris exhibition opening.

fig 109   Signed 'Lotus' mark Clutha Vases c.1888.   Private Collection

fig 110   *The Jeffrey's Workbook* c.1874.   *Courtesy of A. Sanderson & Sons*

It is worth noting that it is Coupers taking action against Webbs, not Arthur Liberty who registered the Clutha name, and presumably would have had more legal justification for complaint. This suggests that Dresser's involvement is as a designer for Coupers, and that he might also have provided advice as to suitable retailers (A.L. Liberty being known to Dresser).

The Liberty Yuletide Catalogue of 1898 confirms Clutha derives from the ancient Roman name for the River Clyde. Throughout industry, Dresser's designs bear titles, see *The Jeffrey's Workbook* reproduced at figs 110 & 115 They may be grouped as Cities; Agra, Cairo; Countries; Egypt, Cyprus; Rivers or seas; Volga, Gulf, Caspian or merely subjects ... Fire, Celtic Knot, Daffodil. Kordofan and Clutha both designed by Dresser and retailed by Liberty would fit such a sequence, and perhaps more comfortably than that of the later Tudric and Cymric sequence usually proposed as promoting a vaguely Celtic or Gaelic inheritance.

fig 111   PODR Registrations 1889, James Couper, Glasgow.
Courtesy of The PRO

Whilst Webb's imitation was presumably titled on their impression of Dresser's sources for the Clutha range, it is quite apparent that Dresser took inspiration from whatever and wherever he thought appropriate. Thus, Clutha includes amongst many others, Peruvian, Persian and Chinese shapes, and glass, ceramic, and bronze exemplars in much the same way as did Linthorpe pottery. Just as Linthorpe is elevated by unique glazes, Clutha glass transcends other art glass by its infinite variety of colour, texture, and irregularity.

Virtually all techniques applicable to glass in its molten state were utilised in Clutha production. Cutting or engraving were not.

Aventurine has been quoted as an essential characteristic of Clutha but it is clear that many examples exist with no aventurine at all.[105]

fig 112   1889 Paris Exhibition, Goodes Stand.   *Courtesy of Thomas Goode and Co.*

It has been noted that many of the most strongly coloured examples of Clutha are those that are most often marked, suggesting early production, and coloured as preferred by Liberty, but more likely as intended by Dresser.

(Footnote 102:   The date, 1880, is quoted by Nellie, Dresser's daughter. Nellie 'entered' the Dresser Studio in 1889 at the age of 18, the year after Clutha was produced. To paraphrase Nellie, her sister Ada was the only serious member of the Studio. Nellie left home in 1904, to become an Anglican deaconess. I do not trust her recollections.)

(Footnote 103:   N. Pevsner. *C. Dresser Industrial Designer Architectural Review LXXXXI* 1937 pp. 183-6.)

(Footnote 104:   Liberty registered 'Clutha' on 6th June 1888. Coupers write on the 29th November 1888, to complain of an *"infringement of their new Clutha range by the Thomas Webb and Sons range of 'Old Roman Glass.' "* Coupers believed this *"was more or less an imitation of 'our Clutha Art Glass' designed for us by Dr. Christopher Dresser... the sale of which we have hitherto confined to Messrs Liberty & Co. and their agents throughout the UK."* (*The Pottery Gazette,* 29 November 1888). More specifically, Coupers continue by claiming Mr Wilkes Webb had purchased *"over a dozen samples after they were first displayed"* in Liberty. Despite 'assurances' from Webbs some 'eight or nine weeks ago' ———- (i.e. in August 1888). The launch of Webb's range of 'old Roman glass' prompted Coupers to complain directly to Messrs Webbs by a letter on the 12th November, to be followed by a very public airing of their case in their letter of 29th November in *The Pottery Gazette.* This prompt, pointed, and public action by Coupers surely suggests protection of a new range of glass.)

(Footnote 105:   H. Newman *An Illustrated Dictionary of Glass,* 1977, p.72.)

Much as Linthorpe, Old Hall, and Ault lack distinction without the controlling hand of Dresser, Clutha after a few years seems to have been restricted to a pale acid green metal streaked with white, bubbled more heavily than early production, and more reliant on aventurine for decorative interest. Certainly some of the shapes illustrated in *The Liberty Yuletide Catalogue* of 1895,[106] are most often found in this colour, compare signed Clutha at fig 113 with 114.

It has not been possible to prove George Walton's connection with Coupers, but the range of glass ascribed to him is also of this pale green metal and is dated to after 1896. The earliest reference to Walton and Clutha is Pevsner 1939.[107]

The only located glass designs by Walton would seem to be those in the Royal Institution of British Architects (RIBA) which are mostly Venetian in manner for an unknown maker.[108]

A possible verification that Walton designed Clutha glass which one might acknowledge is its inclusion in the George Walton corner in the Arts & Crafts Exhibition, 1903 where one would assume he would hardly waste space promoting other artists' work.[109] In addition, examples from the limited range of attributed Walton glass, usually of a more symmetrical nature than Dressers, are often to be seen in illustrations of Walton interiors. They remain very much inspired by Dresser, and Walton must have thought highly of them, to have displayed them so often. One might wonder why Walton's Clutha is so well illustrated, whilst Dresser's examples are so poorly publicised.

The following 1898 Liberty catalogue description would apply to both Dresser and Walton glass at this date

> "the general effect is a rich translucent substance, dispersed with brilliant flashings and whorls, which form a very 'cosmos' of impressionist designs."

It might be noted that this catalogue includes Clutha items for as little as 1/-, in Liberty, and this might go some way to supporting the view that Dresser intended his designs to be available, that is affordable, to as wide a clientele as possible. Even a housemaid could afford such a price on occasion.

Contemporary reference to Clutha glass is sparse. The main coverage is included in the article on Dresser's work in the Studio article of 1898, where 11 glass designs are illustrated. Although this is 11 years after Clutha's introduction, all these contemporary references seem to have been 'lifted' from this article and appear in sequence in the Loetz records of the same year as special designs for Max Emmanuel, London. Loetz examples of these designs are known, especially the 'propeller' vase.

Dating continental 'art' glass is an almost impossible task, most is described 'circa 1900'. If such a date is correct then Dresser's organic shapes with attenuated necks and generally elongated forms would seem to pre-date those of Galle and Daum, and myriad other continental firms.

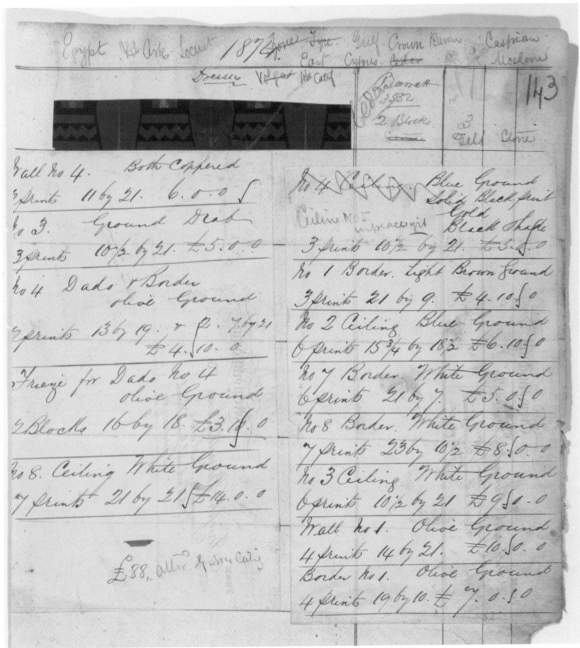

fig 115 A page from *The Jeffreys Workbook* c.1874, The record of a decorative scheme. *Courtesy of A. Sanderson & Sons*

One Daum ewer would appear to be almost directly copied from the Dresser ewer illustrated in Liberty's catalogue of 1895, and the Daum version seems to have continued in production well into the 1920s.

The earliest reference to Tiffany's blown glass, as opposed to window glass, is 1892. Tiffany's 'Jack in the pulpit' vase not only has Dresser's organic verticality but also the same extravagant 's'-profiled lip as the Dresser vases (see fig 106) at Paris in 1889. It is difficult to accept that Tiffany achieved this shape independently of Dresser.

(Footnote 106: See fig 225 W. Halen. Even if by Dresser, are most often found in this colour.)

(Footnote 107: *RIBA Journal* 46.)

(Footnote 108: Some of which are illustrated in *Inspired by Design* Manchester University 1995 as exhibited at the 1903 Arts and Crafts Exhibition.)

(Footnote 109: Reinforced by several items of Clutha donated by Mrs Walton to the V&A.)

fig 116   Attributed Sowerby 'Studio' Vases 1882 - 1888.   *Private Collection*

Sowerby Studio

Unlike Clutha Glass, Sowerby art glass was exhibited at the Art Furnishers Alliance. *"... a distinct variety in art, whilst they display not only the art of glass making, but also the art of glass colouring."* This was *The Pottery Gazette's* report on 1 May 1882.[110] A report in *The Newcastle Daily Chronicle* 21 October 1882, confirms this stating *"Dr Dresser reported most favourably as to its success."* So much is fact. What form such glass took and by whom it was designed must for the present remain a matter of conjecture.[111]

The Laing Art gallery holds the main collection of Sowerby Studio glass, which can be streaky, transparent, opaque, marbled or merely tinted, often asymmetrical, sometimes gourd-shaped, occasionally with trailed and applied work, in fact, very similar to Clutha glass itself. *The Pottery Gazette* quote 'of infinite variety' seems most accurate, but their last reference is less clear. *"Mr Sowerby offers, we hear, these goods as his own designs..."* It may be possible to compare this with A.L. Liberty offering goods as his own designs (i.e. preferring to claim any kudos for himself). After all, even a Victorian trade reporter would know the difference between 'offering his own designs' and 'designed by'.

A choice must be made between provincial Sowerby pre-guessing Dresser by four years and designing a range of glass completely unlike anything seen previously, and that of Dresser determined to produce glass to his own designs,[112] by organising the production of Sowerby with the same concepts of shape and colour used for Clutha. In the prospectus for the Art Furnishers Alliance 1880, mention is made of 'new artistic glass' to be made by the Tees Bottle Company. None seems to have been identified. Perhaps the intended range of glass just never materialised and it took Dresser two years to arrange alternative production by Sowerby. It's interesting to note that Salivati, Burke & Co. and James Powell & Sons were both creditors of the Art Furnishers Alliance, as was James Green & Nephew, the glass and china retailer.

(Footnote 110:   The manufacturer, Sowerby Ellison is also amongst the creditors of the Art Furnishers Alliance.)

(Footnote 111:   See S Cottle; *Sowerby Gateshead Glass* 1986 for moulded and Venetian ranges.)

(Footnote 112:   C.1888 Sowerby closed its studio, the same year as Clutha was launched.)

(Footnote 113:   However, the tumbler in fig 107 is Clutha and does have a pontil.)

(Footnote 114:   See p.119 C.R. Hajdamach *British Glass* 1991.)

(Footnote 115:   C.R. Hajdamach, *British Glass* 1991.)

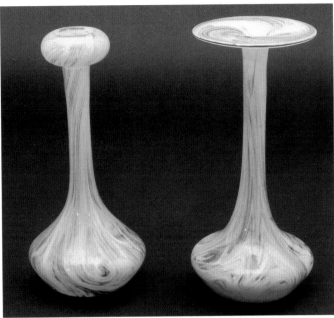

fig 117 Undated Richardson & Sons 'Clutha' type Vases. *Private Collection*

H.G. Richardson and Sons

The similarities between these examples of H.G. Richardson & Sons' work and Clutha are readily apparent; only when handled is it clear that the Richardson's pieces are of a superior lead metal and bear polished pontils. Whilst the smooth surface texture does occur in some examples of Clutha, normally polished pontils do not.[113]

The previously unpublished archive photographs figs 118 & 119, include shapes common to both Richardson and Clutha, and other shapes are obviously 'related'. Although not annotated, or dated, their Richardson's origins are proved by the price codes.[114]

The fact that William Haden Richardson II (1825-1913), a close relation of the Stourbridge Richardson, was manager of the James Couper & Sons factory at the time of Clutha's introduction, provides yet another link, which will only serve to tantalise until accurate dating of this range is achieved.

Scanning reference books for potential Dresser items or those that conform to his principles can be most rewarding. The conical teapot by Richardson for the 1878 Paris Exhibition [115] would be a prime contender for 'pre-Clutha' Dresser design.

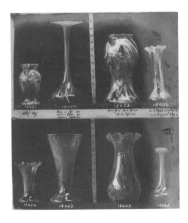 

figs 118 & 119 Undated Richardsons archive photographs. *Courtesy of Broadfield House Glass Museum*

fig 120   *Left*,   Decanter, probably Webb, engraved with Dresser's 'Bluetit' pattern of 1870.
Right,   Carafe, Webb, etched with pattern 11211 in Webb archive 1878.   *Courtesy of D. Bonsall*

fig 121   Webb archive drawing, 1878.   Courtesy of Edinburgh Crystal

Thomas Webb & Co.

The Furniture Gazette praises Webbs bronze glass shortly after its introduction at the Paris Exhibition in 1878. Most of the relevant Webb archive material is dated 1878, and many shapes are annotated 'green bronze' or 'crackled bronze' and occasionally P + P which is taken to refer to Phillips and Pearce, the London retailers. The archive is not complete. Despite the overlap between ceramic and glass design, and allowing for the cribbing of published material,[116] the concentration of so many designs conforming to Dresser's principles in this short span of pattern numbers circa 1878, an exhibition year, seems more than mere coincidence. The fact that one piece of Webb's bronze glass (unfortunately not included in the archive) matches a Dresser sketch in *The Ipswich Sketch Book*,[117] and another [118] Linthorpe shape prior to Linthorpe production goes some way to reinforcing this idea.

It is suggested that Webb's bronze glass may have been inspired by Schlieman's excavations at Troy in the early 1870s. However, it needs a gifted designer to adapt the Troy discoveries to a range of glass which stands in its own right and is not a mere imitation. O' Fallon, the chief designer for Webb is an unknown quantity, and nothing in the Paris Exhibition reports preclude the possibility that the designs themselves may have come from outside Webb.

The pre-Clutha shaped vases fig 126, seem years ahead of anything similar and present a challenge to provide an exemplar in glass which it has not proved possible to meet. 'Bronze etched in gold', fig 121, might be considered 'too elaborate' for Dresser, and in any event, one might argue that didn't Dresser rail against excessive cutting? Certainly, this is the case, but this is 'etching' by mechanical and chemical methods not cutting by hand, and given this, it is hard to disallow Dresser designing 'elaborate' designs for glass, any more than for elaborate

(Footnote 116:   C.R. Hajdamach *British Glass*.)

(Footnote 117:   *The Ipswich Sketch Book*, p.40.)

(Footnote 118:   See C. Manley illustration no.315 confusingly attributed to Richardson.)

fig 122 Cat. G-024

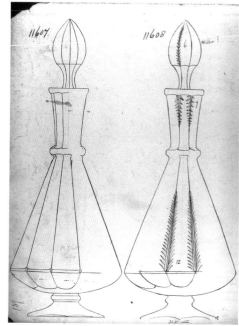

fig 123

fig 124

fig 122 Webb Crystal Decanter 1878. Perhaps a startling proposal as a candidate for 'Dresser' glass, this decanter nevertheless conforms to Dresser's requirements for glass as set out in *Principles*. It is similar in form to a Watcombe jug of c.1872, and the corresponding design is located amongst other 'Dresser' models in the Webb archive of 1878. Doubts as to the modernity of the cutting might be dispelled by comparison with the 'Wheat Ear' pattern by Irene Stevens ARCA for Webb Corbett Ltd, c.1950
fig 123 Webb archive drawing, 1878. *Courtesy of Edinburgh Crystal*
fig 124 *Unity in Variety,* 1860

figs 125 to 129, right, Webb archive drawings, 1878. *Courtesy of Edinburgh Crystal*

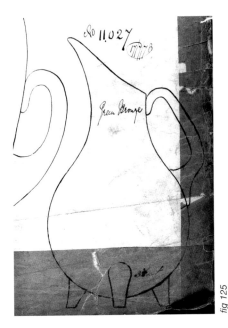

fig 125

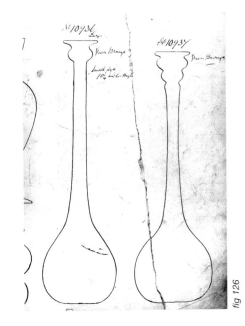

fig 126

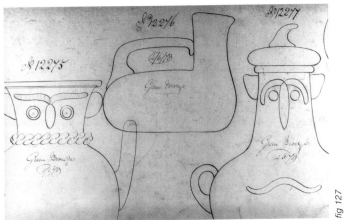

fig 127

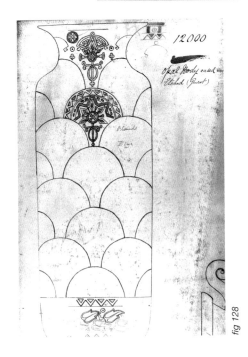

fig 128

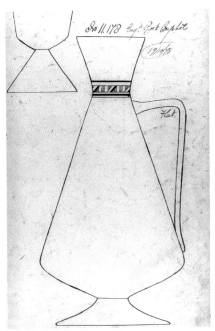

fig 129

fig 130 Webbs Crackled Bronze, 1878.
Private Collection

Minton products, cloisonné for example. Cameo, the glass that glass collectors value most highly, is exactly the type of glass that Dresser considered 'a waste of labour.' A form of cameo that Dresser might well have designed and approved of is illustrated at fig 128, a simple cased vessel with etching sufficiently deep to contrast the two-coloured casings, achieved with minimal effort. The V&A possesses a Webb bronze glass plate with a multi-gilt metal appliqué in Japanese taste which seems to illustrate another method Dresser might have thought legitimate in further enhancing glass.

Examples of bronze glass with enamelled decoration, either on the surface of the glass or etched and infilled, are also known and these too, provide an additional legitimate decorating technique not that far removed from Minton examples. In fact the example at fig 134 bears an exact Minton cloisonné pattern, though it is not claimed here as a Webb production. An additional range of Webb glass, fig 132, [119] of a similar date, also includes shapes that Dresser would not disown, and appears to be the same body as bronze glass but with a softer green iridescence.

Bronze glass seems to have been made for a very short period only, possibly due to health risks from the fumes produced, and by the three firms T. Webb & Sons, Richardson, and Tutbury Glassworks. Richardsons exhibited their own range of bronze glass also at the 1878 exhibition, and then agreed to cease production as Webbs complained of an infringement of their 'patent.' [120] A further Richardson firm, Tutbury Glassworks, advertised as the "sole licensee" for the manufacture of Webb's patent bronze glass" in *The Pottery and Glass Trades Gazette,* September 1879.

(Footnote 119:   Titled 'iridescent' No.179 illustrated by C. Manley.)

(Footnote 120:   C.R. Hajdamach, *British Glass.*)

Cat. G-017.   Cat. G-018.   Private Collection.   Private Collection.   Cat. G-019

fig 131   Webbs Bronze, 1878

fig 132   Webbs Iridescent, c.1878.   *Private Collection*

fig 133   Webbs Bronze enamelled, 1878.   Cat. G-022

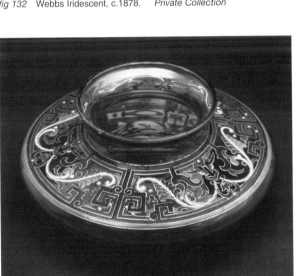

fig 134   Unattributed Vase with Minton Cloisonné pattern, c.1875.
Private Collection

fig 135   Webbs Bronze etched and enamelled, 1878.
Private Collection

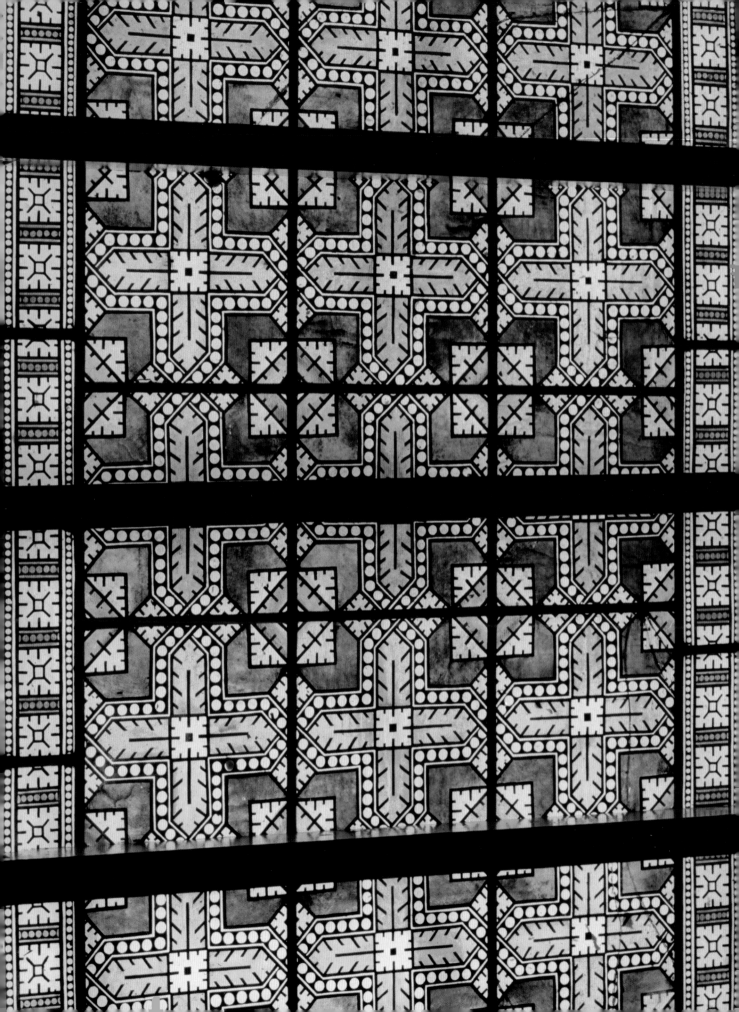

Stained Glass

Dresser sets out in Chapter IX of *Principles of Design* the purposes of a window 'to keep out rain, wind and cold, and must admit light; having fulfiled these ends it may be beautiful.'

It is unlikely that a large amount of 'Dresser' stained glass was produced so we are fortunate that the glass produced for Allangate, around the time *Principles* was written in 1873, remain in situ. Indeed we are doubly fortunate that there is a range of stained glass and settings, which facilitates comparisons and assessment with Dresser's text in *Principles*.

Window

This window (fig 137) is illustrated by Dresser in *Modern Ornamentation* 1886. It overlooks the service yard of Allangate Mansion, a setting corresponding to *"a mass of bricks and mortar"* as quoted by Dresser. It is not large being approximately 18 inches wide. This enabled Dresser to use relatively large sheets of glass, rather than small quarries leaded together, and decorate them by use of one of his highly idiosyncratic 'frost' patterns, which is achieved, it is supposed, by little more than stencil. It is a painted window rather than true 'stained glass' which normally consists of differently coloured glass pieces leaded together.

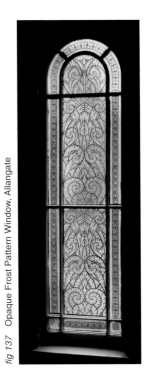

fig 137 Opaque Frost Pattern Window, Allangate

Decorative Roundels

Situated in the drawing room at Allangate there are four such windows as fig 138 with wide ebonised and gilt frames. They were set against *"a cool buff wall, relieved by designs* (stencilled) *in chocolate and gold, above a dado of crimson with floral stencil work in gold and black. In the evening, they can be illuminated by means of powerful gas jets fixed behind as well as being lit in the daytime as ordinary stained glass windows."* [121] These medallions each contain an 'antique' female head, illustrative of morning, noon, evening and night, and conform to Dresser's requirement that *"pictorially treated subjects ... should be treated very simply, and drawn in bold outline without shading."*

The fan lights or over-door panels shown at fig 139, overleaf, are also from the drawing room at Allangate and again are achieved simply, but also illustrate well, Dresser's preferred colour palette especially in the borders, 'tints of creamy yellow, pale amber, light tints of tertiary blue, blue grey, olive russet and other sombre or delicate hues enlivened by small portions of ruby,' (see Footnote 101). These panels are truly Anglo Japanese.

It ought to be pointed out that the subjects for the drawing room windows are chosen with care, and link other features in the room and with the garden (thought to be by Dresser as well). The fireplace, for example, bears the motto in gold upon a black background *'Consider the lilies of the field... they toil not neither do they spin'...* and relates to a medallion showing a woman spinning (itself appropriate for the house of a textile manufacturer), and a fanlight depicts lilies.

fig 138 'Night' glass Roundel, Allangate Drawing Room

fig 136, left   Skylight, Allangate

(Footnote 121: *Castles and Country Houses in Yorkshire* 1885. *Bradford Weekly Telegraph.*)

Skylight

Fig 136 is opaque glass painted grey black and yellow, providing light for the main bedroom corridor and landing at Allangate, larger than fig 137 it is achieved in the same simple and efficient manner. The complicated (and unattractive) roof at Allangate would have been visible had transparent glass been used.

There are other windows at Allangate, for which illustrations are not available, but which should be mentioned here. Over a door to the service yard is another fan light which is leaded in the more orthodox way, and consists of a diaper with tulips similar to those illustrated in figure 176 in *Principles.* A bedroom corridor contains a further skylight leaded in the usual way, but combining strong colours of ruby and blue and yellow.

The description of Allangate written in 1885, (see Footnote 121), includes 'staircase windows, the inner framework being in each case filled with stained glass.' This is unfortunately no longer present. It is tempting to suppose that this consisted of the more elaborate and colourful type of glass as illustrated in figures 174 and 184 in *Principles,* an example of which has not been located.

Bushloe House (date unknown- possibly 1867 or 1876) contains the skylight over the main staircase hall, which is in the same restrained colour palette as the majority of Allangate windows - that is yellow, grey, white and black (fig 164) The series of windows from a now demolished bay window, but retained at Bushloe, and illustrated in Halen, fig 198, present a problem. Three of this series are illustrated in the Cox and Co. catalogue for 1873.[122] It is suggested that these are additions to Dressers' original work at Bushloe House, as is the Jekyll insert to a bedroom fireplace: 1876, (the date Dresser's will was drawn up by H Owston of Bushloe House), would seem a plausible date for this work.

It is interesting to note that *Principles* contains a reference to *"those excellent artists in stained glass, Messrs Heaton Butler and Bayne of Garrick Street"* ... a connection with Dresser that is reinforced by the Dresser designs contained in the album on display in the Exhibition. A further possible link to Dresser may be Campbell, Smith, and Campbell, 85, Southampton Row (stained glass and art tiles mosaics) who are listed as creditors of the Art Furnishers Alliance in 1884.

(Footnote 122: See A. Stapleton Footnote 40 V. Moyr Smith *Decorative Arts Society Journal 20.*)

fig 139 Over Door Panel, Allangate
fig 140, right Allangate Drawing Room Ceiling and Over Door Panel

fig 142   Stool, attributed to Christopher Dresser.   Courtesy of D. Bonsall

Furniture

by Christopher Morley

Furniture by Dresser is invariably described as 'circa 1880-83', 'for the Art Furnishers Alliance' and 'manufactured by Chubb'. This is inadequate and inaccurate. Furthermore it has demoted Dresser's furniture to a less important category (because of its supposed late date) and obscured the fact that Dresser was responsible for complete schemes of interior decoration as advanced and sophisticated and as early as any reforming 'progressive' architect.

Unfortunately, two sets of Dresser furniture with known provenances surfaced early in the days of the rediscovery of Dresser, and both had strong connections with the Art Furnishers Alliance, fostering that attribution and date. These are the dining room furniture, sideboard and hanging corner cupboard,[123] owned by G.H. Chubb (Lord Hayter) and the Bushloe House furniture designed for H.B. Owston. The ascribed attribution and date seem to be based on the following basis:

Firstly, Messrs Chubb and Sons are said to have organised the manufacture of furniture to Dressers design for sale through the AFA.[124] The Chubb archive contains the only known contemporary photographs of Dresser furniture.[125] Secondly, the AFA is the only known retailer of Dresser furniture. Both G.H. Chubb and H.B. Owston were shareholders of the AFA.[126] Thirdly, 'A dado for a library' designed by Dresser for Bushloe appeared in *The Furniture Gazette* in June 26 1880, seemingly confirming the assumed 1880 date for Bushloe furniture.

fig 141, left   Ebonised Chair c.1880-83 for The Art Furnishers Alliance, manufactured by Chubb!   *Private Collection*

(Footnote 123: *Illustrated Victorian Furniture* R.W. Symonds and BB Whineray. 1962 pp 82-83. It has been suggested that, like the now discredited Egyptian sofa from Bushloe, their provenance may not be sufficient evidence to prove authorship to Dresser. The curved apron to the sideboard, and curved outline to the cupboard being at odds with known Dresser furniture.)

(Footnote 124: *Prospectus* Art Furnishers Alliance 1880.)

(Footnote 125: Partially illustrated W. Halen *Christopher Dresser* 1990 pp 58-63.)

(Footnote 126: *Prospectus* Art Furnishers Alliance 1880.)

fig 143 Detail of fig.147. Private Collection

However, Dresser certainly knew Owston as early as 1876, when Owston drafted Dresser's will prior to his visit to Japan. Moreover, Owston married and 'prepared' his new house after its purchase for his Yorkshire bride in 1866.[127] It seems possible that Dresser's work at Bushloe dates from either 1866, or 1876 (the early date being the more remarkable.) The Bushloe furniture is stencilled yet, no reference to stencilled furniture at the AFA has been traced in contemporary literature or in the sale catalogue. No furniture labelled AFA is known either.

Illustrations of furniture by Dresser of a date earlier than 1880 are known, for example, in *Principles of Decorative Design* 1873, though little of this furniture has yet been discovered. Dresser himself refers to a chaise longue designed for a wealthy client which was formed of 'black wood', (and so, presumably made).

By far the most important proof of Dresser furniture being made prior to 1880 is the full account of the near total refurbishment of Allangate, Halifax, in 1870 [128] *'The whole of the woodwork and the furniture... manufactured from special designs prepared by Dr Dresser... is in ebonised wood with incised gold work.'* Where is this furniture now, and who made it?

Greek motifs form the most consistent theme in the decorative scheme at Allangate, the anthemion and Greek key patterns in particular. There exist several undoubtedly 'Dresser' items of furniture that are decorated in this way, and these might be said to be totally consistent with the interiors at Allangate (See figs 143 to 147). None of the bedroom furniture seems to have been rediscovered, but the main bedroom suite is described as being stencilled in grey upon black and with gilt incised work, whilst the remainder was black and gilt incised only.

The geometrical or mathematical proportions of the low chair have been commented on previously.[129] It is suggested this chair comes from the library at Allangate as the incised pattern is similar in both chair and marble fireplace, and that figs 143 to 147 are 'Allangate' furniture also, and thus considerably earlier than previously thought.

(Footnote 127: *The Master Builder* Hiram Abiff Owston D. Sheard Hunt 1991.)

(Footnote 128: *Bradford Illustrated Weekly Telegraph* 1885.)

(Footnote 129: See plate 228 *Nineteenth Century Design,* Charlotte Gere and Michael Whiteway, 1993.)

fig 144

fig 145

fig 146

fig 147

figs 144 to 147,   Furniture totally consistent with interior details at Allangate, 1870.   *Private Collection*

fig 148, left   Bushloe House Frog Suite Wardrobe. Ebonised pine stencilled decoration, c.1866-1876.   Cat. F-001
fig 149   Bushloe House Dressing Table, ebonised pine, and Mirror, ebonised mahogany, c.1866-1876.   Cat. F-003, F-004

fig 150, left Bushloe House Bedside Cupboard, ebonised pine, c.1866-1876. Cat. F-005

fig 151, above Detail from Bedside Cupboard, Bushloe House. Cat. F-005

fig 152, below, Bushloe House Chest of Drawers, ebonised pine, c.1866-1876. Cat. F-002

fig 153, right Detail of Owl from Bushloe House, Lotus Suite, c.1866-1876. Private Collection

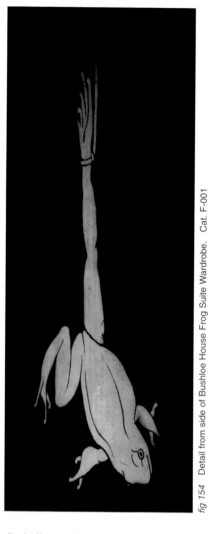

fig 154   Detail from side of Bushloe House Frog Suite Wardrobe.   Cat. F-001

At Bushloe House the interior decoration was an admixture of both Gothic and Egyptian detail, but it also included a Persian dado in the library.(130) It is not surprising therefore to note that some furniture from Bushloe has both Egyptian and Gothic detail as well. The extraordinarily inventive frog suite includes Gothic detail, but defies precise stylistic analysis, as Dresser intended.(131) The dressing table, mirror and chest of drawers from Bushloe are illustrated here for the first time. They have no stencilled decoration, and rely for decorative effect on the geometrically arranged metalwork of the drawer pulls and back plates, both slightly oversized. Only the wardrobe and mirror has a chamfer; plinths are plain and solid, and there are no mouldings. The considered proportions and stark simplicity of this Dresser-designed furniture sharply contrasts to that of standard commercial production.

Bushloe House furniture appears to be constructed of pine; (132) that suggested for Allangate, was mahogany. Whether this choice of material is based upon cost, or shows progression, is yet to be explained. It might be worth noting that pine, whilst as suitable as any wood for stencilling upon, would be less suitable for fine incised work.(133) It is tempting to assume that the 'missing' Allangate bedroom furniture was similar to that at Bushloe. Perhaps the back plates were 'anthemion' or 'star' shaped and the stiles and blank square shaped horizontal members bore Greek key, or zigzag patterns incised, and different suites in different degrees of elaboration.(134)

The AFA furniture is better documented. The photographs in the Chubb archive and the few sketches in the catalogue of stock at the close of AFA give a fair idea of the range of furniture at this later date, 1883. 'Black and gold' and 'ebonised' are the most common description and the illustrations show furniture not too dissimilar to that ascribed here at Allangate, that is with incised lines and dots and with anthemion motifs. More worthy of note is the inclusion of non-ebonised furniture in dark mahogany, walnut, oak and fumigated oak, for rooms such as the library, drawing rooms, boudoir, hall and bedroom. Additionally, there is the use of lattice panels.(135)

Stuart Durant,(136) illustrates sketches of 'grotesques in wood' suggesting that they might have been used for the ends of arms of chairs. A former resident of Allangate has described a large piece of furniture, shelves above, cupboards below, which it is thought was the buffet from the dining room. In addition to a deep pierced frieze; he described such grotesques, with especially sharp teeth, at the intersections of the vertical and horizontal members on the upper part of the buffet. For the benefit of future hunters of Dresser furniture it is pointed out that at the last sighting of this item, it had been 'improved' by the addition of a coat of white gloss paint.

Dresser explains quite clearly his requirements from a furniture manufacturer.(137) Competence in basic joinery allied with low cost seem as important as any other consideration. 'Maximum effect with minimum means.' (138) Local firms rather than London makers would have reduced costs further. It is likely that should Dresser furniture be found labelled, obscure provincial firms will be responsible. However AFA chairs have been noted with 'Liberty' labels. These may be old stock from AFA, or alternatively the continuation of a successful line, taken over by A.L. Liberty who was also a shareholder in AFA.

Allangate and Bushloe are but two fortunate survivals from a list of commissions hinted at but lost to us. J. Ward, the Crossleys, J. Lewis, J. Lister, all manufacturers, all from Halifax, all gave Dresser commissions.

fig 155   Detail of door panel from Bushloe House Frog Suite Wardrobe c.1866-1876.   Cat. F-001

Surely Halifax was not the only town in which Dresser worked. Where are the smart London commissions?

Are we to assume that only textile manufacturers indulged in fashionable decoration, as proposed by Dresser? May we not suppose that Dresser maximised every opportunity presented by his links with industry to propose decorative interiors for them also? What about artistic and fashionable society outside Dresser's trade links?

1865-1883 is suggested as the period when Dresser was most active in furniture design.[139] Moyr Smith refers to furniture designs for Dresser when he joined the Dresser Studio in 1867. Dresser's last known designs for furniture were those for the Art Furnisher's Alliance circa. 1883. A quote from *The Cabinet Maker* in a comment on a Bugatti chair at the Italian Exhibition, 1888, seems to suggest Dresser furniture had not been exhibited publicly for some time.

> *"... reminds one in passing of some of the highly original forms which used to come from the pencil of Dr Christopher Dresser..."*

The furniture from the AFA would appear not that different from furniture commissioned for Bushloe and Allangate or even that illustrated in *Principles*. It was 'off the peg' and not customised nor tailored to fit with Dresser decoration, the choice available must have been thought wide-ranging enough to suit most of their clients' requirements.

The coal box, fig 146, probably designed for Allangate, is illustrated in *The Furniture Gazette,* before the AFA existed. It is also illustrated in the Chubb archive, as is a stool closely related to the chair, fig 145. Nothing here precludes this range from having been designed for Allangate, ten years earlier.

'Other' Dresser furniture is likely to resemble known Dresser furniture in form, and bear decoration achieved by the simplest of means. Whilst ebonised examples seem to have been identified most readily, walnut, oak, mahogany and even pine were used. It should not come as a surprise to find judicious inlay, carving, imported panels, even metal plaques or cloisonné utilised as decoration.

(Footnote 130:   Illustrated in *The Furniture Gazette* 1880, June 26.)

(Footnote 131:   *Studies in Design* 1876, p.14.)

(Footnote 132:   S. Durant, *C. Dresser.* Durant states the colours at Bushloe are like *Studies in Design* 1874-76; that the Owl Suite shows Dresser *"as an orchestrator of colour... the equal of Owen Jones."* The Frog Suite demonstrates this even more clearly.)

(Footnote 133:   Note the sophisticated contrast between the smooth glossy carcass and the rough matt finish of the pattern in fig 150.)

(Footnote 134:   All but one 'enamelled' bedroom suite are described as *"incised"* in the *Bradford Illustrated Weekly Telegraph* 1885.)

(Footnote 135:   Close examination of the lattice panels and other turnings on Dresser furniture reveals bold geometric profiles rather similar to those of W. Burges, rather than the insipid and fussy turnings normally encountered on 'commercial' art furniture.)

(Footnote 136:   *Christopher Dresser* 1993, p.81.)

(Footnote 137:   Letter from Dr Dresser to *The Furniture Gazette* July 24, 1875 referring to *"large second rate, yet good houses"* i.e. manufacturers, quoting twice the price that could be obtained from a local maker to the trade.)

(Footnote 138:   S. Durant *Christopher Dresser* p.41.)

(Footnote 139:   Dresser carried out an interior design scheme for Ward in 1865. This may have included furniture.)

fig 156   Benham & Froud mahogany Coalbox c.1870.
Courtesy of D. Bonsall

Not the most exciting items of furniture, nor the most collectable, coal boxes were an essential item in any room with a fireplace. It is surprising that so few first class Dresser coal boxes have been discovered. Surely fig 146 is not the only Allangate coal box model to have survived? Fig 156 is also quite extraordinary, and would seem to relate to other Benham & Froud designs registered circa 1870.[140] Also the design numbers 240268, 240269, 240419 and 292779, registered in 1871-73. All but the last seem to be registered for shape alone as they appear 'unfinished' and lack handles. The carcass varies in each illustration, mahogany, oak and pine seem to have been used and presumably any could have been ebonised. The illustrations in Durant's *Christopher Dresser* p.78 seem somewhat tame by comparison, though no less likely as Dresser designs. It would appear that the handles were interchangeable, and that Benham and Froud's choice would not necessarily match Dresser's.

If the 'anthemion' decorated furniture at figs 143 to 147 is indeed from Allangate, designed in 1870, and consistent with illustrations in *Principles,* 1873, it is surely deserving of more serious evaluation. Should 1866 ever prove to be the date of the Bushloe House commission, direct comparison with Godwin's earliest aesthetic furniture becomes possible, and the fact that one of Godwin's sketchbooks is annotated *"from drawings of Dr Dresser"* becomes more pertinent and intriguing. It also becomes desirable that both commissions are more thoroughly assessed.

fig 157   fig 158   fig 159   fig 160

figs 157 to 160   Benham & Froud Coalboxes, PODR registrations c.1871-73.   *Courtesy of The PRO*

(Footnote 140: See W. Halen *Christopher Dresser*. fig 55.)

fig 161   Bushloe House 'Marble' Fireplace with possible later insert by T. Jeckyll

Bushloe and Allangate

by Christopher Morley

Interior Design

Whatever date Bushloe House proves to be, such evidence as we have,[141] points to the fact that in general, the furniture was ebonised as at Allangate. In contrast, the woodwork within the main hall, and the curiously panelled doors are in varnished pitch pine.[142] Only one fireplace remains (fig 161) and this is in black 'marble' incised and gilt. The stencilled work in the hall (figs 162 & 165) has probably either been varnished or has discoloured; in any event where 'chipped' the colours are in a much brighter key. The green of the 'waves' for example must surely be blue, discoloured by yellowing varnish. Such encaustic tiles as exist in the hall corridor (fig 163) would at first sight appear to be standard Minton products. Their pattern and arrangement will stand closer examination, which may well prove to be a Dresser product, together with the cast iron grills covering the heating pipes. The lantern top which lights the hall carries an impressive bank of Dresser stained glass (fig 164) which must have cast a warm glow in the hall, reinforced by the varnished woodwork, and one suspects, a tertiary wall colour between the bands of stencilling.

The lush complexity of the dado in the library [143] hints at the richness aimed for in the reception rooms.

(Footnote 141:   Sale catalogue 1942.)

(Footnote 142:   The bedside cupboard illustrated figs 150 and 151, presumably part of a complete suite, relies on the contrast between the ebonised framework and pitchpine panel, as much as on its stencilled pattern. This is an excellent example of Dresser employing highly figured timber in a 'legitimate' manner.)

(Footnote 143:   Illustrated at a later date *The Furniture Gazette* 26 June 1880 in black and white and described as *"Persian."*)

fig 162 Bushloe House Hall stencil

A measure of the transformation possible by the addition of colour can be gauged by comparing the black and white design [144] with the finished coloured version of the ceiling at Allangate bearing in mind this has survived 129 years in an industrial town.

The new south front of Bushloe, in yellow brick with sandstone dressing is curiously difficult to date and no architect has been proposed. Certain features in this new part of the building, the newel post to the staircase, the door panels and the pierced cornice (ventilation grilles?) [145] to the wood construction of the lantern, suggest Dresser's guiding hand, whoever the architect.

Allangate is well described [146] and reviewed [147] and is illustrated thoroughly here. It is apparent that this interior is of international importance, when Dresser's links with America are acknowledged.[148]

Surviving interiors that might usefully be compared are the smoking parlour of the J.D. Rockefeller House New York 1880 and the Grand Veterans Room Seventh Regiment Armoury New York 1879-80. The ebonised woodwork and furniture of the former, and coffered ceiling, stained glass and turquoise tiles of the latter being features in common with Allangate. 'The Peacock Room' by J.M. Whistler and T. Jekyll 1876-7 [149] is

fig 163 Bushloe House Corridor floor

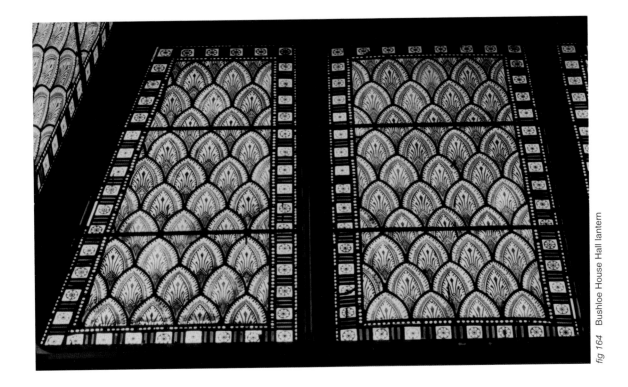

fig 164 Bushloe House Hall lantern

a stunning example of aesthetic decoration, but is not the work of one man, nor the happy collaboration of two. Leighton House London is an exotic blend of east and west, and probably the finest accessible aesthetic interior in this country, but much of what we admire most are afterthoughts, added to the 1866 original at a later date, 1876 - de Morgan tiles, 1877- Arab Hall, 1880- ebonising of staircase. The Green Drawing Room in the V&A 1867 might be considered by some as aesthetic, but in a more correct homespun historicist manner. If there remain other surviving interiors of this style, quality and date they remain to be published. Only in the illustrations provided by E. Godwin for W. Watt's furniture catalogue can we detect interiors with strength and sophistication that Dresser sought and achieved at Allangate.

Much of Dresser's considerable influence in Britain and America was assimilated through his books *Principles of Decorative Design* and *Studies in Design*.[150] Allangate is the manifest embodiment of these exemplary publications, and provides tangible evidence which proves Dresser not merely theorised but practiced what he preached.

fig 165 Bushloe House Hall stencil

(Footnote 144: Illustrated in *Modern Ornamentation* p.11.)

(Footnote 145: Visible W. Halen, *Christopher Dresser* 1990 Ill. 197. These on close inspection are similar to Godwin or Burges escutcheons.)

(Footnote 146: *Castles and Country Houses in Yorkshire* from *Bradford Illustrated Weekly Telegraph* 1885.)

(Footnote 147: H. Lyons *Christopher Dresser Interior Designer. The Decorative Arts Society Journal 21.*)

(Footnote 148: D.A. Hawks *The Decorative Designs of Frank Lloyd Wright* 1979, p.3.)

(Footnote 149: *In Pursuit of Beauty* 1987 Ill. 4.10 also Ill. 4.13 and Ill. 4.22.)

(Footnote 150: *Principles* published in articles in the *Technical Educator* 1872/3, and printed in book form in London and New York, 1873 and *Studies in Design* published in parts and then book form 1874-1876.)

fig 166   Wallpaper Designs c.1865

The Heaton Butler Bayne Portfolio

Cat. X-001

The portfolio of designs from Heaton Butler Bayne displayed at this exhibition contains several designs by Christopher Dresser, and many others attributed to him, c.1865.

The portfolio is known to have been in the possession of the Bayne family (as late as 1972), and one page is marked with a Bayne name and address. Another page is annotated "seen by M. Harrison", a researcher on stained glass. The portfolio was bought at auction by Haslam and Whiteway and later bought by New Century for this exhibition.

The portfolio now contains 40 pages, but three pages with designs by Norman Shaw are known to have been removed. The remaining pages contain

> 7x black and white plates of church windows and two in colour
> 31x mixed water colours, wallpaper cut-outs (some varnished), plus cut-outs from a tile catalogue

It is believed that Heaton Butler Bayne best known for its stained and painted glass entered the interior design market in the 1860s. The portfolio would probably have been either a company reference book, or one for customers to consult.

The portfolio has been photographed and recorded and the photographic record is displayed on view. One page has been disassembled and the designs mounted and framed.

The portfolio is for sale either as an entire item or split into its component parts. Accurate details of the one page, currently framed and mounted, have been kept and it should be a simple matter to restore to its original position.

fig 167

fig 168

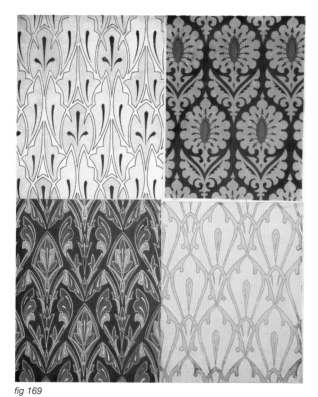

fig 169

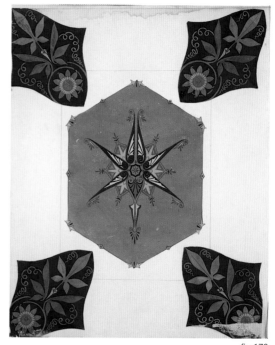

fig 170

fig 171

fig 172 Probable Glass Designs, c.1865

fig 173 Wallpaper Design. *Dresser wrote that wallpaper might not be cut in straight lines prior to pasting*

fig 174 Wallpaper Designs   Detail of Library Ceiling, Allangate
fig 175, *overleaf*

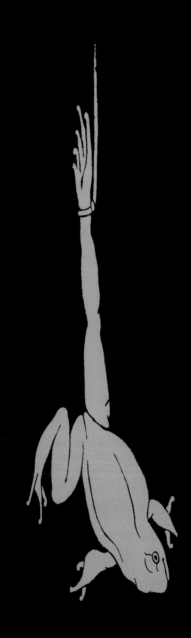

EXHIBITION
CATALOGUE

NEW CENTURY
2ND - 19TH JUNE 1999

PRICE LIST

A grading system is used in this price list to guide purchasers in assessing authenticity. The majority of items made from Dresser's designs were neither signed nor acknowledged.

No items are included in this exhibition unless we believe there is serious reason for suggesting a Dresser attribution. The letter following the catalogue number of each item offers a guide to authenticity, as follows:

A   Dresser. Proved by:

   1. Facsimile signature or other manufacturer's credit
   2. Identical items have been recorded as bearing facsimile signatures or credits, or
   3. A record in contemporary journals or Dresser's notebooks/sketchbooks, or
   4. Carries a provenance to known Dresser commissions.

B   Dresser, but lacking documentary evidence.

C   Considered to be Dresser in that the item is:

   1. Totally consistent with Dresser's principles, or
   2. Manufactured by a known Dresser manufacturer.

D   Demonstrates some Dresser features, but is not totally consistent with Dresser's principles or known Dresser models.

E   Not claimed as Dresser.

New Century staff will be on hand to discuss items should a customer wish advice.

RESTORATION. Where an item is known to be restored, this is declared in the catalogue entry.

CERAMIC RESTORATION has been commissioned where enjoyment of a piece would be degraded if left unrestored, or where a hairline may develop into a running crack if not held.

METAL RESTORATION has been commissioned where a crack or an unstable item renders the piece unusable. In the case of some cruet sets, glass containers have been blown for New Century using traditional methods, to replace missing containers. Commissioned containers are marked "NC 1999". Dresser designed the glass as an integral item of his condiment sets, and an empty container is not what Dresser had in mind. It would render the set neither *"useful nor beautiful"*.

GLASS in the glass section has not been restored, but see G-026.

STYLE OF PRESENTATION. All sizes are to the nearest ¹/₂". Measurements refer to height, unless otherwise stated. The abbreviation D in the text, refers to a Dresser facsimile or manufacturer's credit. T refers to Henry Tooth.

C-047   C-001   C-037

CERAMICS

LINTHORPE

C-001 A   VASE. *10"/25cm. Shape ?58. D.T. Green & white glaze over band of incised decoration. White body. Body crack sealed (3350) see illustration* **£330**

C-002 B   VASE. *4"/10cm. No marks. Attributed Linthorpe/Dresser. Green, brown & white flowing glaze on red body. 4 bosses (4471)* **£160**

C-003 B   VASE. *5"/13cm. Late mark. Shape 1090. Green & brown glaze on white body (4545)* **£360**

C-004 A   VASE. *6"/9cm. Shape 152. D.T. Hand-thrown. Various glazes over ribbed body (4498)* **£550**

C-005 A   SOLIFLEUR. *5"/12cm. Shape 57. D.T. Green glaze over a pyramid shape. Three indents with three rosettes inserted. Green glaze over white body. Rim chip restored (3934)* **£375**

C-006 A   VASE. *4"/10cm. Shape 110. D.T. Green glaze on white body. Bands of 'Dresser' incised decoration. Rim hairline (3938) see illustration* **£280**

C-007 C   VASE. *3"/8cm. Shape 1392. Indistinct marks. Green, white, blue & brown glaze over red body. Two rows of four bosses (4575)* **£100**

C-008 C   VASE. *as above (4576)* **£100**

C-006

C-009 B   JUG. *7.5"/19cm. Shape 826. Late Linthorpe mark, attributed Dresser.* Interesting red glaze brushed into a mid-green over white body. Restoration to rim (4546)
see illustration   **£300**

C-010 A   PLATE. *7.75"/20cm. Shape 656. Clear marks. D.T.* Brown & green glaze over moulded water lily design (4008)
   £300

C-011 B   VASE. *4.5"/11cm. Marks indistinct.* Brown glaze over red body with 5 thumb imprints. Restored rim chip (4061)
   £145

C-012 A   PERUVIAN JUG. *7.5"/18cm. Shape 318. D.T.* Brown glaze over red body (4065)
   £1100

C-013 A   VASE. *3.5"/8cm. Shape 513. D.T.* Ivory glaze with black blossom sprays on white body (3411)
   £180

C-014 A   VASE. *14.5"/37cm. Shape 477. D.T.* Flowing glazes with brilliant depth of colour over red body (4544)
   £1350

C-015 A   VASE. as for C-014. *Unsigned.* Plum & ochre glaze. Spider's web pattern (4637)
   £1350

C-016 A   VASE. as for C-014. *Unsigned.* Plum & green glaze. Reticulated pattern (4638)
   £1350

C-017 D   BOTTLE VASE. *8"/20cm. Shape 200.* The shape is a known Dresser shape, but the decoration is of a later style. The number 2072 was originally Impressed, but was changed to a hand-written 200 all of which is under the glaze (4255)
   £260

C-023   C-024

C-018 A   VASE. *7"/18cm. Shape 159. D.T.* Mixed flowing glazes covering overall incised decoration over red body (3985)
   £580

C-019 A   JUG. *7"/18cm. Shape 665. Late mark,* but other examples known with D.T. marks. Green-yellow glaze over white body. Restored rim chip (4077)
see illustration   **£380**

C-020 A   VASE. *8"/20cm. Shape 218. D.T.* Brown & green glaze on two incised bands of decoration over red body. Restored rim chip (3628)
   £500

C-021 A   VASE. *10"/25cm. Shape 139. D.T.* Ochre top with blue & green glaze over red body (3498)
   £550

C-022 B   BONBON DISH. *5"/13cm diam. Shape 991. Attrib. Dresser.* Green glaze with white veining. EPNS rim & handle. White body (4543)
   £245

C-023 A   VASE. *12"/30cm. Shape 290. D.T.* Brown, ochre & green glaze over water lily moulded design, on white body (4413)
see illustration   **£1680**

C-024 A   VASE. as C-023. Restored hairline (4414)
see illustration   **£660**

C-025 A   VASE. *8"/20cm. Shape 161. D.T.* Ochre top, green middle on incised pattern. White body (3929)
   £550

C-026 A   Bowl. *9"/23cm diam. Shape 415. D.T.* Brown & green band of incised decoration over white body. EPNS rim & handle (4104)
   £550

C-027 B   SOLIFLEUR. *4"/10cm. Marks Indistinct.* Brown & ochre glaze. Rim chip restored (4669)
see illustration   **£120**

C-028 A   VASE. *5.5"/14cm. Shape 168. D.T.* Brown & green glaze on white body. Six thumb indents with rosettes. Restoration to rim (4129)
   £400

C-029 A   VASE. as above. Restoration to rim (4129B)
   £400

C-027

C-030 C   TWO-HANDLED VASE. *22"/55cm. Shape 2330. Late marks.* Honey glaze over white body. Angular handles with undulating terminals (2663)
see illustration   **£2000**

C-031 A   VASE. *8"/20cm. Shape 287. D.T.* Blue & green glaze over red body, standing on four feet. Restoration to rim (3974)
see illustration   **£550**

C-032 A   TWO-HANDLED JUG. *8"/20cm. Shape 337. D.T.* Brown, green & blue glazes on red body. Moulded design (4206)
   £460

C-033 A   TWO-HANDLED JUG. as above (4207)
   £460

C-034 A   OIL-LAMP BASE. *10"/25cm. Shape 652.* Brown, green & blue glazes on red body. Four handles (3856)
   £450

C-035 C   OIL-LAMP. *11"/28cm* of which *3"/7cm* is ceramic base. *Shape 1456.* Brown & cream glazes on red body. Four handles, one restored (1667)
   £400

C-036 A   VASE. *9"/23cm. Shape 35. D.T.* Multi-coloured flowing glaze over red body (3596)
   £500

C-030

C-039

C-037 A   VASE. *10.5"/27cm. Shape 159. D.T.* Brilliant brown & green glaze over incised decoration. Red body (4573)
see illustration   **£850**

C-038 A   JUG. *10.5"/27cm. Shape 877. D.T.* Multi-coloured glaze over red body. Base chip (4367)
    £860

C-039 A   THREE-LEG POT. *18"/46cm. D.T. All marks indistinct.* Green, brown with some red glazes on bands of incised decoration over red body. Ovoid shape on three triangular legs. Leg chips restored & two hairlines sealed & coloured in. Restoration was necessary to save hairlines from running (BC005)
see illustration   **£4000**

C-040 A   DOUBLE GOURD. *8"/20cm. Shape 326. D.T.* Brown, green & blue glazes on red body. Collapsed style (3783)
see illustration   **£550**

C-041 A   DOUBLE GOURD. as above (3784)
see illustration   **£550**

C-042 A   DOUBLE GOURD. as above (4232)
see illustration   **£550**

C-043 A   DISH. *8.5"/21cm. Shape 276. D.T.* Red & ochre glazes over white body. Collapsed style. Restored rim chips (JT020)
    £280

C-044 A   DISH. as above, different colours (4243)
    £280

C-045 A   DISH. as above, different colours (4242)
    £280

C-042   **C-040**   **C-041**

C-046 A   VASE. *21"/54cm. Shape 224. D.T.*
           Various brown & green glazes on
           classical urn; bands of Greek key &
           anthemion. Two handles (4160)
           £1800

C-047 A   JUG. *6.5"/16cm. Shape 784. D.T.*
           Brilliant brown, ochre & various
           blues on red body. Crack around
           base (3110)
           see illustration   **£180**

C-048 A   VASE. *10.5"/27cm. D.* Band of
           moulded leaves. Bands of incised
           decoration. Row of rosettes.
           Restoration to leaves (4668)
           see illustration   **£880**

C-049 A   JARDINIERE. *7"/18cm. Shape 533.
           D.* 2 stylised bands enclosing band
           of orange fruit & blossom. 4
           handles
           £600

C-050 A   VASE. *9.5"/24cm. Shape 24.* Green
           & brown glazes over white body.
           Five thumb presses (3745)
           see illustration   **£480**

C-051 A   VASE. as for C-050. Red body. Ten
           thumb presses. Rim chip restored
           (Misc049)
           see illustration   **£230**

C-052 A   VASE. as for C-050. *D.T.*
           Multi-coloured glazes (4574)
           see illustration   **£600**

C-048

C-053 A   VASE. as for C-050. Blue glazes.
           Reticulated decoration (4622)
           £800

C-054 A   VASE. *8"/20cm. Shape 214. D.T.*
           Multi-coloured glazes over red
           body. Six thumb presses. Minor
           chip to rim (4313)
           see illustration   **£500**

C-051   C-054   C-052   C-050   C-081

C-055   C-056

C-058

C-057

C-062

C-060

C-066

C-055 B   SPLIT-HANDLED VASE. *8"/20cm. Shape 596. Late mark.* Brown & green glaze over red body (4297)
see illustration   **£350**

C-056 B   SPLIT-HANDLED VASE. *13"/33cm. Late mark. Shape 2043.* Brown & green glazes over white body (4464)
see illustration   **£700**

C-057 A   BELL-SHAPED VASE. *9"/23cm. Shape 216. D.* Honey glaze over incised decoration (4235)
see illustration   **£1200**

C-058 A   VASE. *10.5"/27cm. Marks indistinct.* Blue & green glaze over red body (4234)
see illustration   **£650**

C-059 A   VASE. *10"/26cm. Shape 146. Marks indistinct.* Brown glaze over incised decoration (4103)
   £500

C-060 A   NECKLESS VASE. *10"/26cm. Marks indistinct.* Multi-coloured glazes over red body (4465)
see illustration   **£750**

C-061 B   VASE. *8.5"/22cm. Marks indistinct.* Brown & green glazes over red body. Incised & moulded decoration (BC002)
   £550

C-062 A   PLATE WITH MOULDED ROUNDEL. *8"/20cm diam. Shape 353. D.* Multi-coloured, possibly amateur painting & glaze. Flaking restored (4394)
see illustration   **£250**

C-063 A   PLATE. as above (4395)
   £250

C-064 B   VASE, KNOP NECK. *12"/30cm. Marks indistinct* Green glaze on incised decoration (BC001)
   £800

C-065 A   JUG. DOUBLE GOURD SHAPE. *7"/18cm. Shape 594. D.* Brown glaze over white body (4291)
see illustration   **£500**

C-066 A   VASE WITH CRIMPED RIM. *11"/28cm. Shape 167. D.* Brown & green glazes over incised decoration, white body (4508)
see illustration   **£1000**

C-067 A   JUG IN COLLAPSED STYLE. *6.5"/16cm. Shape 342. D.* Brown glaze on floral decoration, red body (4506)
see illustration   **£480**

C-068 A   VASE. *6.5"/16cm. Shape 159. D.* Green brown over red body, incised decoration. Restored rim (4022)
   £220

C-069 A   DECORATIVE FLASK. *12"/30cm. Marks indistinct.* Multi-coloured glazes over red body. Base crack filled & held. Thought to be unique. Rounded handles with undulating terminals (4161)
see illustration   **£1000**

C-069

C-072

C-087

C-086

C-090

C-019   C-065   C-067   C-009   C-031

C-088

C-091

C-070 C   PIN TRAY. LENGTH *3.5"/9cm. Shape 951.* Green glaze, white body (4535)

£75

C-071 B   TEAPOT. *Shape 1651.* Incised decoration, various glazes, white body. Angled spout (4460)

£500

C-072 B   TEA SERVICE. TEAPOT. *Shape 1651.* SIX CUPS & SAUCERS. *Shape 1899.* MILK JUG. *Shape 1703.* Incised decoration, various glazes, white body (4527)
see illustration   **£1200**

C-073 B   TRIO WITH TEAPOT. Lid restored. Decoration as above (4440/4460)

£300

C-074 B   CUP & SAUCER. *3.5"/8cm. Shape 1368.* Leaf decoration, handle in form of a stylised grub. Honey glaze on white body (4621)

£350

C-075 A   DISH WITH JAPANESE HEAD. length *7"/18cm. Shape 293. D.* Green & brown running glaze on red body. One tip restored. The British Museum has a similar shape in silver with Fijian head. Thought to have religious significance (3996)

£2000

C-076 B   MINIATURE VASE. *3.5"/9cm. Shape 850. Marks indistinct.* Clear turquoise glaze on white body (4532)

£140

C-077 C   MINIATURE VASE WITH SQUARE HANDLE. *3.5"/9cm. Shape 850. Marks indistinct.* green glaze on white body (4534)

£100

C-078 B   MINIATURE VASE. *3.25"/8cm. Marks indistinct.* Ochre & green glazes on white body (4533)

£100

C-085

C-079 B   MINIATURE VASE. *3.5"/9cm. Marks indistinct.* Ochre/green running glazes on red body (4531)

£150

C-080 A   RIBBED VASE. *11"/28cm. D. Shape 167.* Blue & green glazes on red body (4496)

£780

C-081 A   DOUBLE-GOURD VASE. *9"/23cm. D. Marks indistinct.* Green & brown running glazes on red body (4499)
see illustration   **£520**

C-082 A   EWER. *8.5"/22cm. Shape 2119.* Green glaze on white body. Shape photographed in Dresser's account book. Restored tip. See fig 55 (3798)
£3000

C-083 A   JARDINIERE. *8.7"/23cm. D. Shape 534.* Brown glaze on red body. 6 split handles & 6 rosettes (4063)
£600

C-084 A   JUG. *8"/20cm. D. Shape 614. D.T.* Brown glaze over white body. Silver rim with inscription *'Arthur's Ale'.* Base chip restored (4688)
£600

C-085 A   EWER. *10"/25cm, including stopper. D. Shape 339.* Abstract bird design with bird's head stopper and curved handle. Brown & green glazes. Thought to be unique (3997)
see illustration   **£3000**

C-086 A   VASE. *10.5"/27cm. D.* Moulded & incised decoration, red body, multi-coloured glazes. Hand coloured. Rim chip restored (3815)
see illustration   **£1250**

C-087 A   VASE. *12"/31cm. D. Shape 105.* Silver rim, Dixon hallmark. Multi-coloured glazes over red body (3878)
see illustration   **£1400**

C-088 A   UNUSUAL TWIN-CHIMNEY VESSEL. *4.5"/11cm. D. Shape 314.* Unglazed terracotta. One chimney restored (4601)
see illustration   **£1200**

C-089 A   PILGRIM FLASK. *6"/15cm. D. Shape 440.* Moulded decoration of Chinese sage on the front, waterfall on reverse, green glaze. Rim chip restored (3879)
£850

C-090 A   MOON FLASK. *6"/15cm. Marks indistinct.* Known Dresser shape. Multi-coloured running glaze, four legs (3860)
see illustration   **£700**

C-091 A   PERUVIAN-SHAPE VESSEL WITH SPOUT AND SWEEPING OVERHEAD HANDLE. *4.75"/12cm. D. Shape 335.* Honey coloured glaze over incised decoration (4582)
see illustration   **£2250**

C-092 A   TWIN SPOUTED PERUVIAN-SHAPE VESSEL. *7.5"/19cm. D. Shape 312.* Brown & green running glazes over moulded decorations. Restoration to 1 spout (4252)
see illustration   **£1000**

C-093 A   DECORATIVE PLAQUE. Diam. *11"/28cm. Marked Linthorpe. D.* Matt grey ground decorated in impasto-technique work. Pink/white wild rose blossoms & green leaves (3742)
£500

C-094 B   CUP & SAUCER WITH TRIANGULAR HANDLE. *2.5"/6cm. Shapes 641/639.* Green & clear glazes on white body
£200

C-092

C-095

C-095 A	FREE STANDING VASE. *19.5"/49cm. D.* Flowing glazes on red body. Body crack held (BC 058) *see illustration* **£2500**
C-096 A	JUG WITH ANGLED HANDLE. *8.5"/22cm. D.* Brown & turquoise glaze over red body (4233) *see illustration* **£2800**
C-097 A	VASE WITH TWO HANDLES. *8"/20cm. Shape 891.* Similar shape seen with facsimile. Square handles, undulating terminals. Rose & brown glazes over white body (4457) *see illustration* **£1000**
C-098 A	VASE WITH CUPPED RIM. *12"/31cm. D.* Green glaze over incised decoration on white body (4324) *see illustration* **£2600**

C-096

C-097

C-098

C-099

C-102

WATCOMBE

C-099 A   VASE. AMPHORA SHAPE, TWO ARCHED HANDLES. *13"/33cm. D.* Green, brown & ochre glazes over red body. Restored handle (BC 067) *see illustration* **£800**

C-100 A   VASE. *20"/50cm. Shape 224. D.T.* Brilliant depth of various glazes on red body. Moulded irises (3933) **£1500**

C-101 A   VASE. *7.5"/19cm. Shape 334. Other marks indistinct.* Front: incised geometric decoration. Back: flowing glazes (4611) **£850**

C-102 A   POT. *4.5"/11cm. D. Shape.* Central column surrounded by 5 onion shapes. Red body. Running glazes (3899) *see illustration* **£2500**

C-103 A   SOLIFLEUR. *5"/12cm. D.T. Shape 849.* Red glaze (4674) **£340**

C-104 C   JUG. *9"/23cm. Not marked* but similar to C-108. Terracotta glazed inside & out, with painted floral decoration. Rim chip. See fig 45 (4276) **£200**

C-105 B   BOTTLE VASE. *7"/18cm. No marks.* Unglazed terracotta moulded decoration, enamelled in blue & black (3688) **£350**

C-106 B   LIDDED JUG. *8.5"/22cm. Marked Watcombe, Torquay.* Terracotta moulded decoration with black & gilt details. Hallmarked silver lid (4583) *see illustration* **£575**

C-107 C   BOTTLE VASE WITH LID & STAND. *11"/28cm. Marks indistinct.* Terracotta, enamelled green, white & black. Greek key design (3897) **£200**

C-108 B   JUG. *9"/23cm. Marked Watcombe, Torquay.* Terracotta, moulded geometric ornament. See fig 45 **£300**

C-114   C-210

C-109 C   VASE. *7.5"/19cm. Marked Watcombe, Torquay.* Stylised boat shape with undulating rim. Moulded decoration. Shape similar to Linthorpe vase identified as "Dresser" in fig 49

£100

C-110 C   VASE. description as above

£100

C-111 B   BEAKER. *3.5"/9cm.* Terracotta, decorated with enamelled florettes (3845)

£120

C-112 D   TOBACCO JAR WITH LID. *3.75"/9.5cm.* Terracotta with blue enamelled band (3714)

£75

C-113 B   JUG. *6"/15cm. Marked Watcombe, Torquay.* Terracotta, moulded ornament. Handle picked out in black & gold. Small chips and rubbing. See fig 45 (4248)

£100

C-114 C   LEMONADE JUG. *7"/18cm.* Terracotta, blue enamel decoration. Restored hairline (3967)
see illustration   **£300**

C-115 B   PIN TRAY. *8"/20cm.* Unglazed. Incised decoration (4600)

£300

C-116 B   URN. *7.3"/18cm.* Terracotta with blue enamelled winged handles. Lid. Finial has been re-stuck
see illustration   **£450**

C-117 B   URN. *8.5"/22cm.* Terracotta. 2 handles comprised of heads & tongues, as in *Principles of Design.* p.122, fig 106. Restoration. See fig 42

£600

C-116   C-106

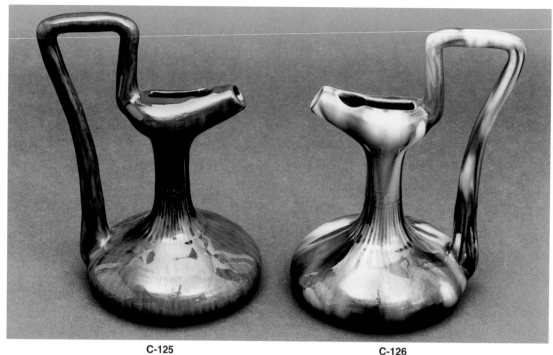

C-125   C-126

AULT

C-118 B   BOTTLE VASE. *7.5"/19cm. No marks.* Brown, green, white glaze over white body (4175)
see illustration   **£350**

C-119 A   VASE, LONG NECK. *10"/25cm. D. Shape 323.* Brown, blue, white glaze over white body. Restoration to rim (3622)
see illustration   **£700**

C-120 A   VASE, TWO HANDLES. *9"/22cm. D.* Green & brown glaze over white body (3185)
see illustration   **£800**

C-121 B   VASE. *9"/23cm. No marks. Identified Dresser shape.* Brown glaze with aventurine, known as sunstone (4514)
see illustration   **£500**

C-119   C-134   C-118   C-120

C-122 B VASE. as C-121 (4513)
see illustration **£500**

C-123 B VASE. *9"/23cm. No marks. Identified Dresser shape.* Sunstone glaze as C-121 (PE003)
see illustration **£250**

C-124 B VASE. as above (PE004)
see illustration **£250**

C-125 A EWER. *7.5"/19cm. Ault logo. Shape 138. Identified Dresser shape.* Brown glaze on white body. Minor rim chip restored (4456)
see illustration **£500**

C-126 A EWER. as above. Green & brown glaze (4291)
see illustration **£600**

C-127 C FLOWER ARRANGER. *6.5"/16cm. Ault logo. Shape 416.* Two shades of green glaze (4455)
£200

C-128 A FLOWER ARRANGER, WITH TWO LUG HANDLES. *4"/10cm. D. Shape 236.* Yellow glaze (3955)
£230

C-129 A FLOWER ARRANGER. *4"/10cm. D. Shape 236.* Red glaze (4619)
£200

C-130 D FLOWER POT. *5"/13cm. Ault logo, Rᵈ· Nᵒ·165933 (1891).* Green glaze on moulded leaf decoration (4505)
£75

C-131 A "GOAT'S HEAD" VASE. *10"/26cm. D. Shape 318.* Rich irridescent green glaze. See fig 20 (4661)
£3500

C-132 A "GOAT'S HEAD" VASE. same as above. Green, white & brown glaze (CL 001)
see illustration **£3000**

C-133 A PAIR OF DOUBLE GOURD SOLIFLEURS. *11.5"/29cm. D.* Yellow glaze (4209)
see illustration **£2800**

C-134 B JUG WITH UPTURNED SPOUT *9.5"/24cm. Ault logo. Shape 176.* Green/brown glaze (4605)
see illustration **£600**

C-135 A "CHINESE MASKS". *9"/23cm. Dresser facsimile.* Green. Restoration to rim (2518)
see illustration **£1250**

C-136 A SMALL FLAT SOLIFLEUR. *4.8"/12cm diam. Dresser facsimile.* Green & brown (4350)
£450

C-137 A SQUAT POT. *6"/16cm. Dresser facsimile.* Blue & brown (4223)
£850

C-138 A FLOWER POT. *8.5"/21cm. Dresser facsimile. Ault logo. Shape 243.* Yellow, moulded decoration (4325)
£850

C-139 C TRIPLE GOURD. *8"/20cm. No marks.* Wavy rim, see picture of Ault fireplace, fig 63. Green & brown (4467)
£550

C-140 C VASE. *7"/18cm. Ault logo. Shape 362.* Small version of stick stand and same shape number. Green & brown (4468)
see illustration **£400**

C-141 C COFFEE POT. *12"/30cm. No marks.* Green & brown, moulded decoration. Restoration to Lid (4296)
see illustration **£900**

C-142 A JARDINIERE. *7.5"/19cm. Dresser facsimile. Shape 322.* Green, four Indians as handles. See fig 64 (4416)
£8000

C-135

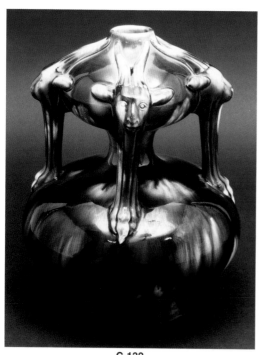

C-132

C-140   C-141

C-133   C-143   C-133

C-122   C-124   C-123   C-121

C-145

MINTON

C-146 B — TEA SERVICE. Porcelain cloisonné blue, gold, chocolate, red & green decoration. 1871. This design was on a piece taken to Japan by Dresser, 1. SIX CUPS & SAUCERS, 2. TWO CAKE PLATES, 3. ONE MILK JUG (4322)
see illustration **£2500**

C-147 B — DINNER PLATE. *10.5"/26cm. Marked Minton. 1872.* Green, black & gold decoration. *Design registered PODR 1862* (4202)
see illustration **£200**

C-148 B — SOUP PLATE. as above (4204)
£200

C-149 C — PILGRIM FLASK. *7.8"/20cm. c.1871.* Porcelain decorated with prunus blossom cloisonné blue. Restoration to rim (2585)
£400

C-150 A — PLATE. *9.5"/24cm. c.1871.* Porcelain. Dresser border is A and recorded in Minton archives. Central decoration added by Minton staff designers (3005)
£300

C-151 B — VASE. *6"/15cm. Indistinct marks. c.1871.* Porcelain, blue cloisonné background (4235)
see illustration **£1150**

C-152 B — GU. *9"/23cm. c.1868.* Porcelain, cloisonné blue background. Restoration to top (4101)
£1500

C-153 B — PAIR OF VASES. *8"/20cm. c.1868.* Porcelain, blue cloisonné background, stylised floral decoration. At some stage an attempt has been made to convert the vases to electric lamps. One has slight restoration to rim, one has hole in base. See fig 31 (4509)
£2750

C-143 A — PROPELLER VASE. *8"/20cm. Dresser facsimile.* Yellow (4378)
see illustration **£1000**

C-144 A — TONGUES VASE. *12.5"/32cm. Dresser facsimile.* Rich red glaze (4690). See fig 65
£5000

C-145 A — GRASS VASE. *22"/56cm. Dresser facsimile.* Rich irridescent green glaze. Some scratches (4349)
see illustration **£2200**

C-146

C-154 B   VASE. *8"/20cm.* Porcelain, blue cloisonné background, Japanese decoration. Hairline to rim, sealed & coloured in. See fig 31 (4028)

£2000

C-155 C   BOWL ON THREE LEGS. *7"/18cm. Date mark 1874.* Porcelain, blue cloisonné background, decoration five cranes in flight. Restoration to one leg (4387)
see illustration   **£800**

C-156 B   BOWL. *7"/18cm. c.1871.* Porcelain, stylised decoration, blue cloisonné background. Base crack sealed (4012). See fig 77

£800

C-157 C   BOWL WITH THREE LEGS. *6.5"/16cm.* Porcelain. Stylised decoration on blue cloisonné background. Restoration to rim (4184)

£700

C-158 C   TOILET SET. ONE EACH JUG, BASIN, SLOP, SPONGE DISH, TOOTHBRUSH DISH AND SOAP DISH. *Registration mark for 1872.* Earthenware. Stylised design in gold, pink, black & ivory (4585)
see illustration   **£1200**

C-159 A   CYLINDER VASE ON THREE SQUARE LEGS. *7.5"/19cm.* Earthenware. Ivory ground. Band of stylised daisies. Design is annotated *"Dresser"* in Minton archives. Small hairline in rim, held & painted (4442). See fig 81
see illustration   **£2800**

C-160 D   TEA CADDY ON FOUR BUN FEET. *4"/10cm.* Porcelain, blue stylised decoration, Chinese characters. Restoration to lid (4100)

£700

C-161 D   TEA CADDY. as above, but pink. Restoration to lid (4199)

£900

C-162 B   MINIATURE VASE. *4"/10cm.* Porcelain, mon decoration, blue cloisonné background. Small base chip (4540)

£400

C-163 B   TRIO. CUP *3"/7.5cm,* SAUCER *5.5"/14cm diam.* SIDE PLATE *7.75"/20cm.* Porcelain, decorated stylised floral motifs on blue cloisonné ground (4066)

£500

C-164 C   SAUCER. Porcelain, Greek key pattern decoration on blue cloisonné ground (3453)

£45

C-165 D   DISH. *9.25/24cm diam. Registration mark for 1872.* Earthenware. Cranes & waves in blue (4002)

£120

C-155

C-151

C-167   C-168   C-147

C-158

C-166 D   PLATE. *10.5"/26cm diam. Year mark 1883.* Design of cranes in blue. Earthenware
                                           £100

C-167 B   PLATE. *6.5"/16cm diam.* Porcelain, richly decorated and gilded on cloisonné blue ground. The plate has been broken & pieced together
see illustration   **£100**

C-168 D   SAUCER. *5"/12cm diam.* Porcelain, oriental motifs on blue cloisonné ground
see illustration   **£40**

C-169 D   CUP AND SAUCER Floral motifs on porcelain (4224)
                                           £100

C-170 B   CUP AND SAUCER. *Indistinct marks.* Stylised floral design on blue cloisonné. Some rubbing. c.1871
                                         £150

C-171 A   SPILL VASE. *4.7"/12cm. Marks indistinct.* c.1865. Three legs. Band of stylised Herb Robert. This vase is sketched & commented upon in *The Ipswich Sketch book,* p.20. Annotated as being in the Italian Court, 1862 Exhibition. This precedes the earliest known cloisonné. Hairline held & coloured in (4672)
see illustration   **£1200**

C-159

C-171

C-184   **C-183**

OLD HALL

C-172 D   Cᴜᴘ. *3"/7.5cm* ᴀɴᴅ Sᴀᴜᴄᴇʀ. Porcelain. Stylised decoration on blue ground. See fig 58 (4443)

                                                £300

C-173 A   Pʟᴀᴛᴇ. *9"/23cm. D.* Earthenware. Hampden pattern. Thumb presses for condiments
        see illustration   **£200**

C-174 A   Pʟᴀᴛᴇ. *8"/20cm. D.* as C-173, no thumb presses
                                      £140

C-175 A   Pʟᴀᴛᴇ. as C-174
                                      £140

C-176 A   Pʟᴀᴛᴇ. as C-174. No facsimile
                                      £150

C-182   **C-179**   **C-180**   **C-181**

C-188   C-187   C-187   C-188

C-177 A	PART DINNER SERVICE, 2X VEGETABLE DISHES, 6X SOUP PLATES. Shanghai pattern (4193) *see illustration* **£1200**
C-178 C	ORIENTAL COFFEE POT. *13.75"/35cm.* Earthenware. Moulded and enamelled decoration (3674) *see illustration* **£650**
C-179 B	JUG. *6.25"/16cm.* Earthenware. Square sided on four feet. Stylised floral decoration (4068) *see illustration* **£550**
C-180 B	JUG. as above. Hairline (3943) *see illustration* **£150**
C-181 B	JUG. *6.75"/17cm.* As C-179 (3942) *see illustration* **£400**
C-182 B	JUG. *7"/17cm.* As C-179 (4275) *see illustration* **£1500**
C-183 B	TOILET JUG. *12.5"/31cm. Registration mark indistinct.* Earthenware. Stylised anthemion decoration (3923) *see illustration* **£600**

C-184 D	TOILET JUG. *13"/33cm.* Earthenware. *Shape graded B* (3386) *see illustration* **£850**
C-185 B	TUREEN (NO LID). *12"/32cm length.* Earthenware. Decoration stylised peacocks (4152) *see illustration* **£350**
C-186 B	TUREEN (NO LID). Smaller version of C-187 (4153) **£200**
C-187 C	PAIR OF VASES. *12"/29cm.* Earthenware. Squared cylinder with elephant heads (3970) *see illustration* **£700**

C-185

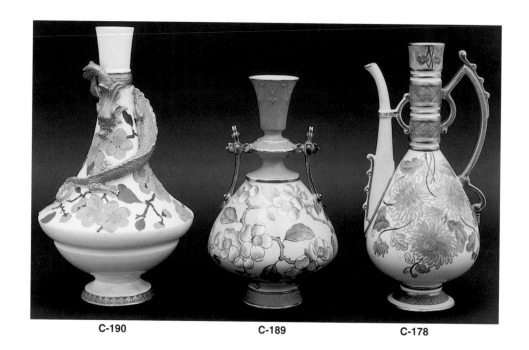

C-190 C-189 C-178

C-188 D PAIR OF VASES. *8.75"/22cm.* Earthenware. Shaped with elephant heads (3253) *see illustration* **£500**

C-189 C VASE. *12.5"/33cm.* Earthenware. Moulded handles. Bold prunus design on turquoise (2222) *see illustration* **£500**

C-190 D VASE. *14"/36cm.* Earthenware. Stylised prunus decoration with moulded gilt dragon around neck (1922) *see illustration* **£400**

C-191 A PLATE. *6.7"/17cm.* Earthenware. Shanghai pattern. Crack (4194) *see illustration* **£45**

C-192 A SIX PLATES. *9"/23cm.* Earthenware. Shanghai pattern. The blue has rubbed off in this colourway *see illustration* **£600**

C-193 C TOILET SET. *Shape & design B. Colouring D.* Earthenware. Eureka pattern. 2x JUGS AND BASINS (1 pair cracked) 2x CHAMBER POTS 1 EACH SLOP, TOOTHBRUSH HOLDER, SPONGE AND SOAP *see illustration* **£800**

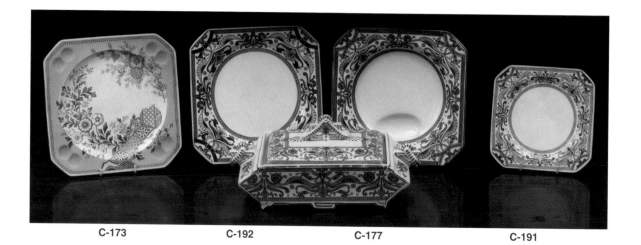

C-173 C-192 C-177 C-191

C-193

BROWN-WESTHEAD MOORE

C-194 D   SANDWICH SET (PART). Porcelain.
           Registration mark for 1868.
           4 PLATES, 1 CAKE STAND (3738)
           see illustration   **£220**

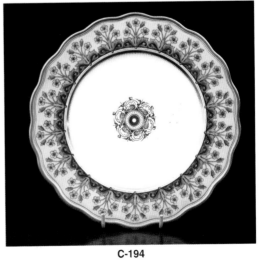

C-194

C-198

C-199　C-202

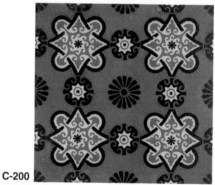

C-200

C-205　C-195

C-196

TILES

C-195 A 8x TILES. *8"/20cm. Minton. Dust pressed. c.1875.* This design is in *Studies in Design* (4335)
see illustration **£1200**

C-196 B TILE PANEL. 4x TILES. *8"/20cm square. Minton.* c.1875 (4069)
see illustration **£1000**

C-197 B TILE PANEL. As above (4069)
£1000

C-198 B TILE PANEL. 2x TILES *6"/15cm square.* 2x TILES *3"/7.5cm x 6"/15cm. Minton.* c.1875
see illustration **£250**

C-199 B 4x TILES. *6"/15cm square. Minton. Dust pressed.* Stylised floral design (4420)
see illustration **£400**

C-200 B 30 TILES. *6"/15cm square. Minton. Dust pressed.* Stylised geometric design. Varying condition (4624)
see illustration **£1200**

C-201 D RUN OF 12 TILES. *6"/15cm square. Some marked Minton, some Minton Hollins* (4625)
£500

C-202 D ENCAUSTIC TILE. *6"/15cm square.* Stylised floral pattern, mauve ground. *Marked Minton* (4626)
see illustration **£150**

C-203 D ENCAUSTIC TILE. as above (4627)
£150

C-204 B WALL TILE. *8"/20cm square. Minton* c.1871. Stylised birds & bulrush design (4624)
£250

C-205 D WALL TILE. *8"/20cm square. Minton* c.1871. Cranes & stylised flowers. Sepia & ivory
see illustration **£100**

VILLEROY & BOCH, GERMANY

Villeroy & Boch have no evidence of a Dresser connection. Villeroy & Boch date the tiles as c.1890. We, nevertheless, suggest a Dresser link.

C-206 D RUN OF 4 TILES. *6.75"/17cm square.* Geometric design, unglazed (4616)
see illustration **£400**

C-207 C TILE PANEL. 4x TILES *6.75"/17cm square.* Egyptian motif design. Smear glaze. Marks V. B. Mettlach (4618)
see illustration **£500**

C-208 D TILE PANEL. as above. Stylised geometric design (4617)
see illustration **£500**

C-207   C-206   C-208

G-001

GLASS

FELIX SUMMERLEY BY JF CHRISTY, LAMBETH

G-001 E   CARAFE. *6"/15cm. Summerley monogram & marked R. Redgrave. Clear glass with plant decoration. c.1847 (4515)*
see illustration   **£2000**

CLUTHA BY COUPER & SONS, GLASGOW

G-002 A   BOTTLE VASE. *7"/18cm. Lotus mark. Brown with white streaks (4237)*
see illustration   **£2500**

G-003 A   SOLIFLEUR. *8"/20cm. Unmarked, but see Liberty Yuletide Catalogue, 1895. Pale green with gold streaks and bubble inclusions. Stylised flower top. This shape has been seen signed (4470)*
see illustration   **£2500**

G-004 A   VASE. *9.5"/24cm. Lotus mark. Green with lighter opaque inclusions. Free triangular form (4162)*
see illustration   **£5000**

G-005 A   DISH. *9"/23cm diam. Lotus mark. Lime yellow with brown swirls and silver inclusions (4089)*
see illustration   **£1000**

G-006 A   WAISTED VASE. *3.5"/9cm. Lotus mark. Green with swirls and bubble inclusions (4090)*
see illustration   **£1400**

G-007 B   BOWL. *4.75"/12cm diam. Unmarked, but see Liberty Yuletide Catalogue 1895. Lime yellow with prunts (3853)*
see illustration   **£1000**

G-008 D   BOWL. *6"/15cm diam. James Couper & Clutha marks. c.1900. Pale green with wavy rim (4200)*
see illustration   **£550**

G-009 A   BOTTLE VASE. *10"/25cm. Lotus mark. Brown with pattern of yellow whorls (4629)*
see illustration   **£9500**

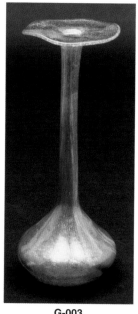

G-003

G-004

G-009

G-008   G-007   G-002   G-006   G-005

G-015   G-014   G-016   G-013

G-010 A   TALL SOLIFLEUR. *15.75"/40cm.* *Lotus mark.* Rose with silver and gold inclusions (4287)
see illustration   **£6500**

G-011 B   'S' LIP VASE. *7"/18cm. Unmarked,* but see *Liberty Yuletide catalogue,* 1895. Green with gold inclusions. See fig 106
    £4500

THOMAS WEBB

G-012 C   VASE. *8.75"/22cm. Unmarked.* Rounded form. Blue bronze. Crackled (CM001)
    £2500

G-013 C   JUG. *4.5"/llcm. Unmarked.* Bronze glass (CM010)
see illustration   **£700**

G-014 C   VASE WITH HANDLES. *3.5"/9cm. Unmarked.* Bronze glass (CM009)
see illustration   **£700**

G-015 C   JUG. *5"/13cm. Unmarked.* Bronze glass (CM008)
see illustration   **£700**

G-020

G-021   G-023

G-016 C   VASE. *5.5"/14cm. Unmarked.*
          Bronze glass with stylised face
          (CM005)
          see illustration   **£900**

G-017 C   MINIATURE VASE. *1.5"/4cm.*
          Unmarked. Bronze glass. See fig
          131 (CM012)
                                      £500

G-018 C   MINIATURE VASE. *4"/10cm.*
          Unmarked. Bronze glass. See fig
          131 (CM011)
                                      £500

G-019 C   MINIATURE VASE. *3"/7cm.*
          Unmarked. Bronze glass. See fig
          131 (CM013)
                                      £500

G-020 C   VASE. 6"/15cm. *Unmarked.* Bronze
          glass. Ribbed (CM007)
          see illustration   **£900**

G-021 C   VASE. *6.5"/17cm. Unmarked.*
          Bronze glass (CM006)
          see illustration   **£900**

G-022 C   BOWL. *7.5"/19cm. diam. Unmarked.*
          Blue bronze glass. Enamelled with
          Japanese decoration. c.1878. See
          fig 133 (CM003)
                                      £1800

G-023 C   JUG. *9"/23cm. Unmarked.* Bronze
          glass (CM005)
          see illustration   **£1800**

G-024 B   JUG. *10.5"/27cm. Unmarked.* Clear
          crystal with wheat ear motifs.
          Compare Watcombe jug. See fig
          122 (CM002)
                                      £2000

G-010

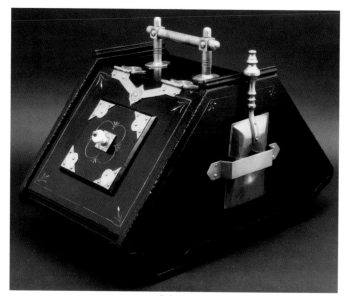

F-007

Furniture

F-001 A WARDROBE. *83.5"/212cm x76.52"/194cm.* Ebonised pine. Stencilled decoration of frogs. 3 compartments: 2 hanging compartments, 1 compartment for drawers. Long mirror.

PROVENANCE: *purchased at sale of contents of Bushloe House, Leicester, in 1942, then by descent until 1998. Bought by New Century for this exhibition.*

Date between 1866-1876. See figs 4, 148, 154, and 155

POA

NOTE Few pieces of Dresser furniture with a verifiable provenance have come on the market in the last 40 years. We can think of only 2 other wardrobes from Bushloe House, both of which bear lotus decoration; one of these was erroneously described as a silver cabinet. Both are currently held in collections.

F-002 A CHEST OF DRAWERS. *37"/94cm x46.5"/118cm.* Ebonised pine with brass drawer pulls. Original blue sugar paper linings to drawers. Ensuite with F-001.

PROVENANCE: *as for F-001. '526' chalked in one drawer. This corresponds with Lot 526 in Bushloe House Sale Catalogue.* See fig 152

POA

F-003 A DRESSING TABLE. *31.5"/80cm x45.3"/116cm.* Ebonised pine with brass drawer pulls (as for F-002). Original blue sugar paper linings. *'337' chalked in one drawer,* as per F-002 above . See fig 149

PROVENANCE: as for F-001

POA

F-004 A DRESSING TABLE MIRROR. *38"/96cm x28"/66cm.* Ebonised pine and mahogany. See fig 149

PROVENANCE: as for F-001

POA

F-005 A BEDSIDE CABINET. *31.5"/80cm x 14"/35cm.* Ebonised pine with stencilled pitch pine panel to door. Brass handle. Compare handle to 'frog' pot cupboard in Jeremy Cooper's book *Victorian and Edwardian Furniture,* p.132.

PROVENANCE: as for F-001. *This item indicates that a third suite exists. Dresser did not approve of highly figured woods because they interfered with the unity of an item. When used, as here, contained within a framework of ebonised wood, their use was considered legitimate.* See figs 150 and 151

POA

F-006 E   DOUBLE BED. Ebonised pine.

PROVENANCE *This was described as a French ebonised bed in the Bushloe sale catalogue. We do not think that Dresser designed this bed. However we believe that at some stage this century the bed was altered and the top of another piece of Dresser furniture was added to the headboard*
see illustration   **£2000**

F-007 C   COAL SCUTTLE. Ebonised pine. Gilt decoration. Brass shovel, a later addition. c.1880 (4409)
see illustration   **£1000**

F-008 C   COAL SCUTTLE. Oak. Original shovel. Brass fittings. c.1875 (4518)
see illustration   **£1200**

F-009 D   COAL SCUTTLE. Benham & Froud plaque of mixed metals. *Frame bears label of Knight & Son, Bath* (4525)
   £1000

F-010 B   COAL SCUTTLE. *Perry label.* Oak construction. c.1885 (4427)
   £1000

F-011 B   COAL SCUTTLE. Benham & Froud plaque of mixed metals on ebonised carcass. Brass fittings. Scuttle probably original
   £1000

F-012 B   HAT AND STICK STAND. *76"/193cm. Coalbrookdale.* c.1869. Black, re-painted. Spine welded
   £4500

F-013 B   STICK STAND. *40"/102cm, Coalbrookdale.* c.1870. Black, re-painted. Repair to rail
   £2800

F-014 B   CHAIR. *34"/86cm. Coalbrookdale.* c.1870. Wooden slats to seat and back restored. Red undercoat
see illustration   **£2500**

F-015 C   BOUDOIR SAFE. *48"/122cm. Chubb label.* Steel. c.1880. Decorative panel and carcass restored. See fig 79
   £3750

F-006

F-016 C   FIREPLACE INSERT. *38"/96cm (H) x40"/102cm (W). Attributed to Coalbrookdale and Minton (back is still intact)*
see illustration   **£3000**

F-014

F-008

F-016

T-006

T-001

TEXTILES

T-001 B   FRAGMENT OF CARPET. *from Allangate, Halifax.* c.1871
see illustration   **£250**

T-002 B   FRAGMENT OF CARPET. as for *T-001*
£200

T-003 B   FRAGMENT OF CARPET. as for *T-001*
£200

T-004 B   TRAY CLOTH. *31"/87cm x24"/ 60cm.* Linen. Attributed to J. Wilson, Belfast
see illustration   **£800**

T-005 D   PAIR OF CURTAINS. c.1870. Brown, grey & yellow. Maroon cotton lining. Original fringing. See background to fig 149
£1000

T-006 B   TERRY QUILT. c.1880. Probably by Barlow & Jones. Lotus design
see illustration   **£1000**

T-007 A   HANGING (FRAGMENT). c.1872. Wool & silk. This design was exhibited by J. Ward, Halifax at the 1872 London Exhibition. See fig 103
£3000

T-004

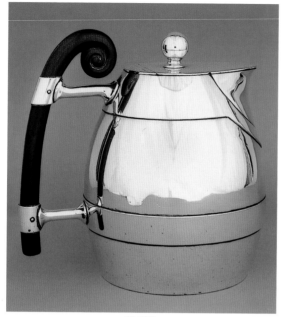

M-002

METALWORK

All silver items are plated except where stated

RICHARD HODD

M-001 B HOT WATER JUG. *5.5"/14cm. Manufacturer's marks.* Plated, ebonised handle. The handle for this jug is shown in *The Ipswich Sketch Book.* Date of manufacture probably 1872-1876. See fig 76 (4312)

£1500

ELKINGTON & CO. LTD

M-002 A WATER JUG. *6"/15cm. Manufacturer's marks.* Shape 16594. R$^{d.}$ N$^{o.}$ 22869. Annotated 'Dresser' in *Elkington Work Books.* Wooden handle, curled top. *Year mark 1890 (4653) see illustration* £7500

M-003 C CRUET. *6.25"/15.5cm. Manufacturer's marks.* Shape 16097. 4 PIECE CRUET, SALT, PEPPER, MUSTARD, VINEGAR, WITH MUSTARD SPOON. *Year mark 1880*

£1000

M-004 B TEA SERVICE. *manufacturer's marks. Shape 15184.* KETTLE AND STAND, TEAPOT, SUGAR & MILK. The shape of the sugar basin is illustrated in *The Ipswich Sketch Book. Year mark 1882* (4679). See fig 70

£10000

M-005 B 3 PIECE CRUET. *5"/13cm. Manufacturer's marks.* Pepper pot original. Salt & mustard glass blown for New Century 1998. T bar handle. *Year mark 1898 (4176)*

£900

M-006 B 3 PIECE CRUET. as above. Original glass. *Year mark 1933 (4707)*

£1200

M-007 B SALT CONTAINER. *2"/5cm. Makers' marks. Shape 287. Year mark 1872.* Gilt inside, (4590). See fig 74

£800

M-008 B/C OIL AND VINEGAR HOLDER. *7"/18cm. Manufacturer's marks. Shape 18309. Year mark 1886.* Without bottles. Metal T bar handle (4655)

£200

M-009 B DOUBLE BONBON DISH. *5"/13cm. Manufacturer's marks. Shape 17618. Year mark 1927.* Re-plated handle. A similar signed example by Hukin & Heath is in this exhibition (4656)

£800

M-013   M-012

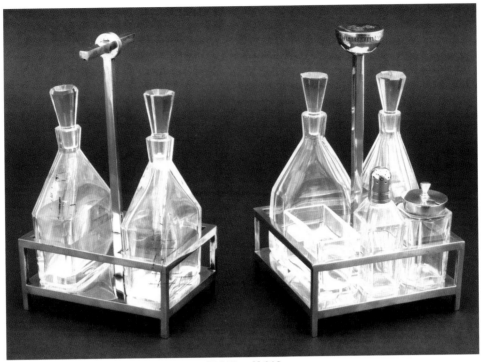

M-017   M-016

M-010 C   CRUET. *3"/7.5cm. Manufacturer's marks. Shape 14244. Year mark 1933.* With ball feet, double loop handle, 2 spoons (4657)
£450

HUKIN & HEATH

M-011 A   3 PIECE CRUET. *4"/10cm. Manufacturer's mark. Shape 1867. D. R$^{d.}$ mark for 1878*
£1000

M-012 A   BONBON DISH. *2.75"/6.5cm. Manufacturer's mark. Shape 2074. D.* (4370)
see illustration   **£1000**

M-013 B   SPOON. *Sterling silver. Marks indistinct. Hallmarked 1882.* This spoon was designed to fit on dish M-012 (4658)
see illustration   **£300**

M-014 B   SUGAR BASIN & TROWEL. *8.5"/12cm. Manufacturer's mark. Shape 2299.* Ebonised handle to basin & trowel (4158)
see illustration   **£1000**

M-015 B   BONBON DISH. *6"/15cm. Marked Goldsmiths & Silversmiths Co. No manufacturer's mark* (4075)
£1000

M-016 A   FIVE PIECE CRUET. *8.5"/20 cm. Manufacturer's marks. Shape 1918. D. Year mark 1878* (4286)
see illustration   **£4500**

M-017 B   OIL & VINEGAR SET. *8.5"/20cm. Shape 1953* (4139)
see illustration   **£2500**

M-014

M-018

M-018 A   TOASTRACK. *5.5"/14cm. Manufacturer's marks. R$^{d.}$ N$^{o.}$ for 1878.* Two rows of spikes (4506)
see illustration   **£2800**

M-019 A   BONBON DISH. *5.25"/13cm. Manufacturer's marks. Shape 2223. D.* (4452)
see illustration   **£2250**

M-020 C   THREE PIECE CRUET. *6"/15cm. Manufacturer's mark.* Trefoil base, 3 ball feet (RW012)
see illustration   **£600**

M-021 B   FOUR PIECE CRUET. *5.5"/14cm. Manufacturer's mark.* Geometric shape. *Shape 2540 or 2550* (3889)
see illustration   **£2000**

M-022 C   FOUR PIECE CRUET. *6.75"/17cm. Manufacturer's mark.* Quatrefoil base, 4 ball feet. Bottles facetted. *Shape 2592* (2082)
see illustration   **£1000**

M-023 A   SIX PIECE CRUET SET. 6 bottles, 2 with metal lids, pepper is original, others have been blown by traditional methods for this exhibition. *Manufacturer's mark. Shape 1996. R$^{d.}$ mark 1878*
   £4500

M-024 B   EGGCUP HOLDER & 2 EGGCUPS. *5"/13cm. Manufacturer's & retailer's marks. Shape 2018.* T bar handle. 2 depressions possibly for eggs. Compare depressions for condiments in Old Hall dinner services
see illustration   **£1500**

M-025 C   EGGCUP HOLDER & 4 EGGCUPS. *5.75"/14.5cm. Manufacturer's mark. Shape 1974.* T bar handle (4105)
see illustration   **£550**

M-026 C   EGGCUP HOLDER & 4 EGGCUPS. *Shape 1974.* As above (4454)
   £550

M-027 B   EGGCUP HOLDER & 4 EGGCUPS. *6.5"/16cm. Shape 1974* but T bar handle attached to base with ball & circular fitting. Space to hold egg-spoons at base of central column (4447)
   £750

M-028 B   EGG WARMER WITH CROW'S FOOT LEGS. *8"/ 20cm. Manufacturer's marks. Shape 2875.* Incised decoration. *Purchaser's monogram* (4364)
see illustration   **£2000**

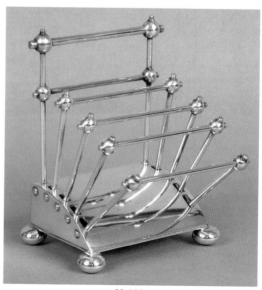

M-033

M-022   M-089

M-029 A	THREE PIECE TEA-SET. TEAPOT, MILK JUG, SUGAR BOWL. *Manufacturer's marks. D. Shape 1888. R$^{d.}$ mark 1878.* Curved legs including one supporting spout. This feature received special notice in a review of the launch of Hukin & Heath's new showrooms at Charterhouse Street, London. See fig 81 (3577) *see illustration* **£10000**

M-031 C	TOAST RACK. *5.2"/13cm. Manufacturer's mark. Shape 2752.* Stirrup handle. Seven uprights. Engraved stylised plant design. 4 bun feet (2984) *see illustration* **£650**

M-032 C	TOAST RACK. *5"/12cm. Manufacturer's marks. Shape 2554.* Fixed sections, 4 ball feet (4284) *see illustration* **£1550**

M-030 B	TOAST RACK. *4.75"/11.5cm. Manufacturer's marks. Shape 2556.* Balls at intersecting angles, fixed sections, 4 bun feet. Recently replated. *R$^{d.}$ mark for 1881.* See fig 83 (BC066) **£800**

M-033 B	LETTER RACK / BOOK END. *5.75"/14cm. Manufacturer's marks. Shape 2555. R$^{d.}$ N$^{o.}$ for May 1881.* Collapsible sections, 4 ball feet (4382) *see illustration* **£1200**

M-019   M-021   M-020

M-028

M-029

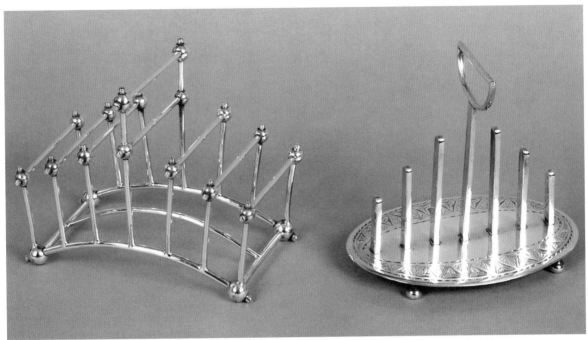

M-032   M-031

M-025   M-024

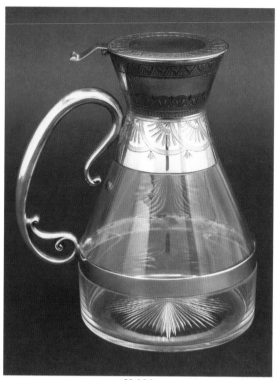

M-034

M-035

M-037

M-038

M-034 A CLARET JUG. *8"/20cm.* Curved plant form handle. Metalwork incised with geometric & stylised forms. *Manufacturer's mark. D. Shape 2085. See fig 82 (4406)*
see illustration **£12000**

M-035 B CLARET JUG. *9"/23cm. Manufacturer's marks. R$^{d.}$ mark for 1881.* Long-necked facetted crystal glass jug with square ebonised handle & plated metal fittings. The facets in this jug compare with facets found in condiment sets (4541)
see illustration **£1800**

M-036 B CLARET JUG. *8.7"/22cm. Manufacturer's marks. R$^{d.}$ mark for 1881.* Long-necked clear glass jug with ebonised handle & plated metal fittings. See fig 84 (4588)
£1750

M-037 B CLARET JUG. *8.7"/22cm. Manufacturer's marks.* Extra long-necked clear glass jug, plated metal fittings & handle (4492)
see illustration **£2000**

M-038 C CLARET JUG. *8"/20cm. Manufacturer's marks. Shape 2521.* Short-necked clear glass jug with metal handle & fitments
see illustration **£1000**

M-039 B PICNIC SET. *Manufacturer's marks. Retailer's mark, Leuchars & Son, London & Paris.* TEAKETTLE & STAND, TEAPOT, METHS HOLDER, MILK FLASK, 3 TRAYS INSIDE ORIGINAL PICNIC BOX. *Stamped Countess of Onslow on outside* (4178)
see illustration **£2500**

NOTE this set was put together on the instructions of Leuchars & Sons and would also have contained 2 ceramic cups, saucers & plates as in the V&A example. The spoons & tongs in this example are not thought to be Dresser

M-040 B CONDIMENT SET. *3.8"/10cm. Manufacturer's marks. Shape 1882. R$^{d.}$ N$^{o.}$ for 1878.* Geometric shaped base, 6 straight legs, round finial on column
£1000

M-041 C TRAY. *13.2"/33cm diameter. Manufacturer's marks. Shape 2079.* Circular tray. 3 ball feet on straight legs. oriental handles (4145)
£1000

M-042 C RECTANGULAR TRAY. *16"/40cm x10.5"/26cm diam. Manufacturer's marks.* Rounded edges. Ebonised handles. See fig 70
£1000

M-039

M-043

M-044 D GLASS TUMBLER HOLDER. *7.5"/19cm. Manufacturer's marks. Shape 2606.* Stirrup handle. 6 holders, glasses not original (2997)
£650

M-045 D CAKE-STAND. *9"/23cm. Manufacturer's mark. Shape number thought to have been double stamped* (4578)
see illustration **£400**

M-046 A PICNIC TEAPOT. *4.5"/11cm. No manufacturer's mark. Retailer's mark Leuchars & Son, London & Paris.* Handle re-plaited. Re-silvered. This shape has been seen with Dresser's name (4211)
see illustration **£400**

M-047 A PICNIC TEA KETTLE. *4.5"/11cm. No manufacturer's mark. Shape 5457, thought to be an error. Retailer's mark Leuchars & Son.* Re-silvered, handle re-plaited. This shape has been seen with Dresser's name (4211)
see illustration **£500**

M-048 B DOUBLE BONBON DISH. *5"/13cm. Manufacturer's mark. Shape 2523.* 2 round dishes joined at handle on 4 straight legs
see illustration **£850**

M-043 D BONBON DISH. *7"/18cm. Manufacturer's marks. Shape 2179.* Frame modelled as bamboo in the Japanese taste, holding a glass dish. Hukin & Heath held an exhibition in 1879. Dresser selected certain Japanese objects for reproduction. The shape number falls within the group associated with Dresser (3059)
see illustration **£450**

M-046   **M-047**

M-048

M-049 B   DOUBLE BONBON DISH. *5"/13cm.*
manufacturer's mark, Shape 2527.
2 oval dishes joined at handle on 4
straight legs. Some surface pitting.
Purchaser's monogram, 1883
see illustration   **£800**

M-050 C   MILK JUG. *2.3"/5.5cm.*
Manufacturer's mark. Shape 2196.
Round handle (4288)
see illustration   **£350**

M-051 C   CHOCOLATE POT & SUGAR BOWL.
Manufacturer's mark. Shape 1997.
Replacement finial on chocolate
pot (4289)
see illustration   **£800**

M-052 C   COFFEE POT. *8"/20cm.*
Manufacturer's mark. Shape 2604.
Plaited handle (4273)
      £500

M-053 B   SERVING SPOON. *9"/24cm.*
Manufacturer's marks. Curved tip
to handle (4591)
      £350

M-045

M-049

M-050   M-051   M-051

M-054 D   Pot with lid. 4"/10cm. *Manufacturer's marks. Shape 1831.* Punched design, mixed metals. Design incorporating Kashmiri & Persian designs. Hukin & Heath had an exhibition in 1879. Dresser selected certain Kashmiri & Persian objects for reproduction. The shape falls into the group associated with Dresser. Re-gilded, as originally sold, since photograph fig 80 (4610)

£300

M-055 D   Dish. *13"/33cm. Manufacturer's marks. Shape 2221.* We cannot date this with confidence, but the shape number puts it well within the Dresser range (4521)

£350

M-056

M-056 A/D   Tantalus. *Manufacturer's marks.* Ebonised handle. D, on Pt A frame (4405)
see illustration   **£5000**

NOTE this design was registered with cut glass decanters. A similar example was sold at Christle's in 1991. We are not certain whether these bottles are original, or when they were made. We think also that plain decanters would be closer to Dresser's ideas. The inclusion of decanters, in any event, make it a useful object. Without decanters it is neither *"useful nor beautiful"*

M-057 A   Soup tureen with ladle. *12"/31cm. D. Manufacturer's marks. Rᵈ mark for 1878.* Round tureen on 3 legs with ivory finial & handles. Separate liner (4490)
see illustration   **£10000**

M-058 B   Fruit knife & fork. *6.5"/17cm. Manufacturer's marks.* Ebonised handles
see illustration   **£500**

DIXON

M-059 A   Toastrack. *3.5"/8.5cm. D. Manufacturer's marks. Shape 67.* Square handle above oriental pattern (JT001)
see illustration   **£5500**

M-060 B   Toastrack. *5.5"/14cm. Manufacturer's marks. Shape 66.* T bar handle above triangular sections (4177)
see illustration   **£5000**

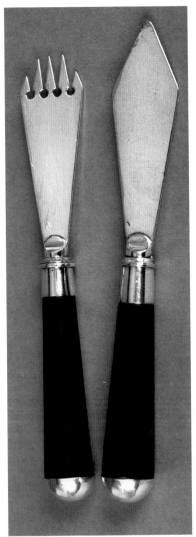

M-058

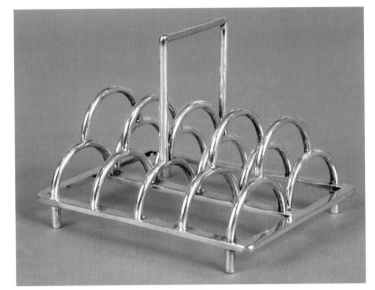

M-059

M-060

M-065

M-057

M-061

M-061 A   BISCUIT BARREL. *7"/18cm. D. Manufacturer's marks. Shape 2891.* 3 straight legs, metal finial & handle. See figs 77, 85, 88 (3988) *see illustration*   **£10000**

M-062

M-062 A   3 PIECE TEA SET. TEAPOT, MILK JUG &
SUGAR BASIN. *D. Manufacturer's
marks.* Incised stylised floral
design. Squared metal handles
with ivory insets. This set is
thought to have come through the
London rooms in the 1980s, and
was exhibited by Leah Roland,
New York, in 1995. It is the only
copy of this design that we have
seen (4512)
see illustration   **£10000**

M-063 C   CRUET SET. *3"/8cm. Manufacturer's
marks.* Ball feet, circular handle.
Compare Elkington M-010
      £400

M-064 A   CLARET JUG. *9"/22cm. D.
Manufacturer's marks. Shape
2554.* Long necked clear glass
jug with metal fittings & handle
(BC 006)
see illustration   **£5000**

M-065 A   SUGAR BASIN. *3.5"/9cm. D.
Manufacturer's marks. Shape
2294.* 4 curved legs. Metal &
ebonised squared handles.
Original owner's monogram (4507)
see illustration   **£1750**

M-064

M-066

M-066 A   TOAST RACK AND EGGCUP HOLDER. *6.7"/17cm. D. Manufacturer's mark. Unusual mark NC 1115.* Squared sections, rounded handle with twist decoration. Detachable eggcups with twist stems. This design was photographed by Pevsner from Dresser's notebook. The shape Number is not one we understand, and may indicate a 'one off'. This is the only example of which we have seen or heard (4481) *see illustration* **£20000**

M-067 C   EGGCUP HOLDER. *8.5"/22cm. Manufacturer's marks.* Four eggcup holders looped together. Supported by four legs joined at the top. Spoons missing (4675) **£2500**

M-068

BENHAM & FROUD

M-068 C ORIENTAL COFFEE POT. *9.5"/24cm. Manufacturer's mark. $R^{d.} N^{o.}$ 114566.* Ebonised handle & finial. Copper. Restored
see illustration **£1200**

M-069 B BRASS AND COPPER TEAPOT. *8.75"/22cm. Manufacturer's mark.* Scalloped & petal shaped trimmings to collar of vessel, applied brass, & scalloped brass handle
see illustration **£2500**

M-070 C BRASS TEAPOT. *7.5"/18cm. Manufacturer's mark.* Angled handle, plaited. Shaped spout. Ebonised finial (4180)
£600

M-071 C COPPER AND BRASS TEAPOT. *8.5"/22cm. Manufacturer's mark. $R^{d.} N^{o.}$ 151114. for 1890.* Copper body, brass spout, finial & handle (BC065)
£600

M-073

M-072

M-069

M-072 C	WATERING CAN. *10.5"/26.7cm.* Copper. *Manufacturer's mark.* Hexagonal body, shaped & curved handle (4503)
	see illustration **£750**

M-073 B	EWER. *14.5"/36cm.* Brass & copper. *No manufacturer's mark.* Double curved brass handle & flower finial. Curved upper body & spout (3231)
	see illustration **£1000**

M-074 C	PAIR OF SMALL BRASS VASES. *5.2"/13cm. Manufacturer's mark.* Crested fluted rims. Incised decoration, straight legs with ball feet (4608)
	£500

M-075 C	TRAY. *19"/49cm length.* Mixed metals, copper, pewter & brass. *Stamped Patent N$^{o.}$ 6886. (Registered 1885 by Benham & Froud)* (3679)
	£750

M-076 C	TRAY. as for M-075 (3437)
	£750

M-077

R. Perry, Son & Co. Wolverhampton

M-077 B   Chamber stick. *3.75"/9.5cm.* Painted iron. Shape composed of 2 interrelated circles. Fully marked (4055)
see illustration   **£700**

M-078 B   Large Brass ewer. *24"/60cm. No manufacturer's mark.* Loopover handle. See Back Cover (4491)
     £8000

M-079 B   Watering can. *8"/20cm. No manufacturer's mark.* Spun brass. Double curved handle. Straight spout. Handle fixed between base & rim. See fig 18 (4474)
     £2000

M-080 C   Brass jug. *10"/25cm. Manufacturer's mark.* Angled handle. Decorated with 3 incised lines on body (4631)
     £250

M-081 B   Chamber stick. *5"/13cm.* Copper. *No manufacturer's name.* Funnel shaped body, decorated with 8 punched rondels. Angled & twisted handle. *Marked Liberty & Co. R$^{d.}$ N$^{o.}$ 133226.* This probably once had a ceramic sconce (3829)
     £300

M-082 D   Chamber stick with brass match holder. *7"/18cm. No maker's mark.* Tubular candle holder attached to wooden handle. 4 ball feet. Match holder separate (4486)
     £500

Henry Fearncombe & Co. Wolverhampton

M-083 C   Jug. *8.5"/22cm. Manufacturer's mark.* Spun brass. Square lip. Ebonised handle. Compare Watcombe jug. See fig 45 (BC061)
     £500

M-084 C   Jug. *8.5"/22cm. Manufacturer's marks.* V shaped lip. *'C.D.' stamped on base.* See fig 45
     £500

A. Kenrick & Sons Birmingham

M-085 B   Stand for iron. *9"/23cm. Manufacturer's mark. R$^{d.}$ N$^{o.}$ 15023 for 1884.* Iron composition with intricate patterning. 2 stops for securing iron (4660)
see illustration   **£450**

M-085

M-093   C-216

MISCELLANEOUS

X-001 B   PORTFOLIO OF DESIGNS. This is fully
             discussed in the text of the
             catalogue. We believe most of the
             designs are by Dresser
                                    £30000

X-002 A   WALLPAPER. 20 rolls of wallpaper
             from the Gemini design in *The
             Jeffrey & Co Workbooks* for 1867.
             Manufactured in 1999 for this
             exhibition.
             see left   *Price per roll,* **£100**

X-003 A   BATHROOM WALLPAPER. a repeat of
             a wallpaper designed by Dresser
             for Steiner, probably reproduced
             c.1965. Suitable for framing. See
             fig 24
                                    £50

ADDENDA

C-209 A   AULT. SOLIFLEUR. *4"/10cm. D.*
             Flattened pyramid. Blue and brown
             (4678)
                                    £850

C-210 B   WATCOMBE. JUG. Silver lid, bands of
             moulded decoration (4700)
                                    £400

C-211 B   WATCOMBE FLOWER POT. *6"/15cm.*
             Turquoise glaze over incised
             bands of decoration on white clay.
             Circular Watcombe marks (4584)
                                    £600

C-212 B   MINTON   BOWL.   *6.5"/16cm.*
             Porcelain. Band of blue with
             stylised decoration. *Painters marks*
             c.1871 (4692)
                                    £280

C-213 C   MINTON   RING   VASE.   *8"/20cm.*
             Porcelain. 2 intersecting circles
             in white glaze. Compare Linthorpe
             fig 49
             see illustration   **£500**

C-214 E   FELIX SUMMERLEY CUP & SAUCER.
             c.1847 (BC068)
             see illustration   **£400**

C-215 E   FELIX SUMMERLEY SANDWICH plate.
             c.1847 (BC069)
             see illustration   **£200**

C-216 B   AULT   JARDINIERE.   *8.5"/22cm.*
             Egyptian style *Shape   189*
             Compare M-093 by Benham &
             Froud
             see illustration   **£680**

C-217 C   MINTON TILE. *6"/15cm.* Stylised
             snowdrops
                                    £180

C-213

G-025

C-218 B   LINTHORPE MINIATURE EWER. *3.2"/8cm. Shape 850.* Red & yellow glaze on white body (JT027)
£150

C-219 A   OLD HALL PART DINNER SERVICE. Shanghai pattern, blue and other colours on ivory ground. Over sixty pieces
see illustration   **£6500**

C-220 B   PAIR OF MINTON LAMPSHADES. Cloisonné pattern. *11.5"/29cm. Shape 508. Impressed Year mark for 1875.* See Joan Jones, *Minton* p.111 for a vase of almost identical pattern taken to Japan by Dresser in 1876. One shade has a hairline
£2500

M-086 A/C   BENHAM & FROUD BRASS AND COPPER KETTLE ON BRASS STAND. The kettle is the same model as photographed for Pevsner. The stand carries $R^{d.}$ $N^{o.}$ *165334, for 1891,* at a time when Dresser was designing for Benham & Froud. Kettle graded A, Stand graded C. See fig 77
£1200

M-087 B/C   BENHAM & FROUD BRASS AND COPPER KETTLE. The kettle has $R^{d.}$ $N^{o.}$ *151114, for 1890.* IRON STAND WITH COPPER FLOWERS *attributed to Benham & Froud.* Kettle B, Stand C
£1000

M-088 C   KENRICK DOORPULL. *Manufacturers marks* (4699)
£230

C-219

M-090   **M-091**

M-093 B   BENHAM & FROUD JARDINIERE. *9.5"/24cm.* Brass foundation, copper patination. *Manufacturers marks.* Compare Ault Jardiniere C-216
see illustration   **£5000**

M-094 B   ELKINGTON SIX PIECE CRUET. *Shape 17282. R$^{d.}$ N$^{o.}$ 24947 for 1885. Year mark 1887.* Six straight legs, T-bar handle. Glass containers commissioned using traditional methods
     £5000

M-095 B   ELKINGTON JUG. *8"/20cm. Year mark 1902.* Squared handle with decoration. Finial as for M-002
     £2800

G-025 D   POSSIBLY WEBB JUG. *6.5"/17cm.* Clear glass with *VR Monogram* (4697)
see illustration   **£650**

G-026 A   CLUTHA JUG. *D.* See fig 108
     £4500

NOTE The handle of this vase where it joins the top of the vase has 'sprung'. It has been filled with a material used in ceramic restoration. Sprung glass can occur after manufacture. The glass itself has not been tampered with

M-089 A   HUKIN & HEATH 6 PIECE CONDIMENT SET. All containers have been commisioned in 1999 for this exhibition. See also M-023
see illustration   **£4000**

M-090 B   HUKIN & HEATH SALT CELLAR. *2"/5cm diam.* Silver, 3 ball feet
see illustration   **£180**

M-091 D   DIXON CLARET JUG. *9"/23cm. Shape 2549.* Ebonised handle, V shaped lip (4589)
see illustration   **£1000**

M-092 A   PERRY CHAMBERSTICK. *5"/12cm. D.* Brass. Snuffer is not original (3541)
see illustration   **£800**

M-092

C-214   **C-215**

F-017

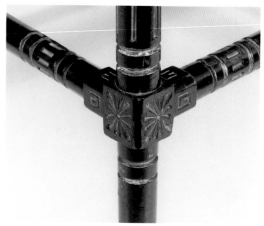

detail of F-017

G-027

G-027 C   CLUTHA FRUIT BOWL. *No marks*
see illustration   **£1000**

F-017 B   W. BOOTY, LONDON. CHAIR.
36"/91cm. Ebonised, gilded
decoration c.1870, possibly earlier
(BC070)
see illustration   **POA**

NOTE W. Booty was active throughout
the 1860s as a cabinet maker and
upholsterer. If a date of 1867 or
earlier can be attributed, this furniture
would pre-date Godwin's Anglo
Japanese furniture

T-008 B   TABLECLOTH. *96"/244cmx36"/91cm.*
Linen damask. Attributed to J.
Wilson, Belfast
see illustration   **£3000**

T-008

STOP PRESS

C-222   C-224   C-223

Figs 33, 41, 43 & 50 appear courtesy of D. Bonsall. We apologise for the omission.

Photograph titled M-090 should read M-052.

Thanks to Road Runner Construction for exhibition display. 0181 742 9292

LATE ENTRIES

C-221 C WATCOMBE TEAPOT. *4"/10cm.* Squared handle, moulded decoration. Brown and tan on red clay. Firing fault and one rim chip (4716)

         £460

C-222 A LINTHORPE VASE. *9"/23cm. Shape 24.* Red and ochre glazes (PE007)
see illustration   **£480**

C-223 A LINTHORPE VASE. *6.5"/16cm. Shape 912.* Unsigned, two handles with undulating terminals. Turquoise blue glaze
see illustration   **£500**

C-224 A LINTHORPE PLATE. *8"/20cm diam. Shape 353.* Multi-coloured roundel with butterfly feature on tan field. Small bruise to rim
see illustration   **£380**

C-225 B 28x MINTON TILES. *6"/15cm.* Brown & cream. Average condition good
see illustration   **£1000**

C-225

G-028

M-097

M-096

M-098

G-028 C	WEBB BRONZE GLASS. *5.5"/14cm.* Unmarked. Stylised face *see illustration*	**£900**
G-029 C	COUPER CLUTHA SOLIFLEUR. *10.5"/27cm.* Unmarked	**£880**
T-009 C	WARD, HALIFAX, (ATTRIBUTED.) Silk on wool. Mediocre condition, some tears. Wine red and gold.	**£250**
F-018 D	SHOP MIRROR. *23"/58cm x 19"/48cm.* Mahogany arched frame. Band of layered Dresser decoration on good quality mirror glass	**£500**
M-096 B	DIXON JUG. *8.5"/22cm. Manufacturers marks. Shape 2522.* Sphere with cylinder neck. Squared handle, 4 ball feet and finial *see illustration*	**£5000**
M-097 B	ELKINGTON MILK JUG. *2.5"/6cm.* Four straight legs. PODR Reg. No. 22864 (1885) Year mark for 1885 *see illustration*	**£800**
M-098 A	HUKIN & HEATH SOUP TUREEN & LADLE. *7.5"/19cm, 12"/30cm diam.* PODR Reg. No. for 1878 Ebonised handle and finial. Ebonised ladle *see illustration*	**£8500**
M-099 B	BENHAM & FROUD FIRE IRON RESTS. *6.5"/16cm.* Brass. An identical pair to this has been seen with manufacturer's marks *see illustration*	**£550**
M-100 D	KENRICK WALL MOUNTED POT HOLDER. Iron	**£250**

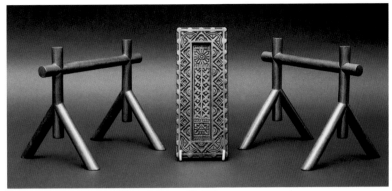

M-099   M-101

M-101 B   KENRICK LETTER BOX FRAME.
               (4718)
               see illustration   **£300**

M-102 C   GASOLIER BY JOHN HUNT & CO.,
               BIRMINGHAM.   *45"/115cm.*
               Rd No. for 1875. Converted for
               electricity. Brass. Many Dresser
               decorative motifs. Structure
               corresponds with Dresser's
               writings on gasoliers in
               Principles of Design.
               see illustration   **£8500**

X-004 B   WATERCOLOUR. Cut out of
               dragon from Heaton Butler &
               Bayne portfolio (q.v.). Frame by
               Richard Murby modelled on fig
               138. Sale conditional on sale of
               X-001
                                          £550

X-005 B   WATERCOLOUR. as for X-004,
               above
                                          £550

M-102

C-220
see catalogue

C-220
see catalogue

M-023
see catalogue

F-012
see catalogue

M-094
see catalogue